D1008545

Charlie McCarthy
Chief Operating Officer
Tetley USA, Inc.
"John's common sense approach and experience in dealing with human nature, complex business problems and solid marketing intuition is a refreshing approach."

Richard E. Goodspeed
President and Chief Operating Officer
The Vons Companies, Inc.
"John has delivered yet another fascinating look at life. We could all benefit in some form or another from his outlook on the world."

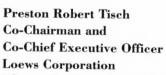

Preston Robert Tisch
Co-Chairman and
Co-Chief Executive Officer
Loews Corporation
"Capozzi's "If You Want The Rainbow . . . " is chock full of lively, interesting, easy-to-read quotes quips and maxims, all offering valuable professional and personal advice. It's a winner!"

Joseph P. Viviano
President and Chief Operating Officer
Hershey Foods
"I always enjoy humorous books and classic one liners and I think yours will be successful."

If You Want the Rainbow You Gotta Put Up With the Rain

---- ♦ ----

500 Secrets for Success in Business

John M. Capozzi

Published By
JMC Industries, Inc.
125 Brett Lane
Fairfield, Ct 06430
1997

Library of Congress cataloging-In-Publication Data

Capozzi, John M.
If You Want The Rainbow You Gotta Put Up With The Rain
500 Secrets For Success In Business / John M. Capozzi
First Edition

p.   cm.
ISBN 0-9656410-0-7
1. Career development.   2. Career Development—Quotations,
maxims, etc.   3. Management—Quotations, maxims, etc.

First Edition
March

This book is dedicated to
businesspeople everywhere
...may they enjoy what they are doing,
learn to do it better,
and prosper from doing it well.

Also By John M. Capozzi

'Why Climb the Corporate Ladder When You Can
Take the Elevator?"

FOREWORD

In 1994 I was approached by a literary agent who wanted to write about my successful business career, specifically about my 13 corporate promotions in 13 years. He suggested I write a "How To" book for anyone trying to get ahead in corporate life. What evolved was a wonderful book which I called, "Why Climb The Corporate Ladder When You Can Take The Elevator?" Rather than write a traditional "How To" book, which has already been done so many times by so many people, I opted to capture my business philosophy through a collection of business maxims.

For almost 30 years I have created and collected business maxims as a hobby. Several in my collection were coined by famous, successful people, others by regular folks and, unfortunately, the source of many is unknown.

This book "If You Want The Rainbow You Gotta Put Up With The Rain", is an extension of my first book. It contains some of the best maxims in my collection. Most are fun and insightful. I am particularly pleased that based upon my own business experiences, I was able to personally create several hundred of the maxims contained in both my books. If anyone in corporate life follows the wisdom of the maxims collected in this book, their odds for success will be far greater.

I have made a lot of money in my business career and many people have told me how "lucky" I have been. But success in business isn't about luck, it's about hard work and careful planning. I do not believe in the success theory of "being in the right place at the right time". Tireless persistence and creativity have put me in a position to find the opportunities I could easily and totally have missed had I been at the beach.

One of the most significant keys to success in business is having the right attitude. Some call it a "winning" or a "positive" attitude. Everything flows from it. Banks or investors feel more comfortable lending money to someone who communicates success. Clients or prospects want to work with a person who is a winner. Business colleagues always prefer to be associated with someone with a positive attitude. A winning attitude allows you to keep going in the face of difficulty.

My winning attitude and desire to achieve financial success have driven me my whole life. When I was ten years old I started selling soda at a construction site across from my home. Throughout high school I shoveled snow every winter, worked in construction every summer, set bowling pins at a local YMCA in the evenings, and somehow found time to be active in sports and get my homework done. My college life wasn't any easier. I attended college on Tuesday, Wednesday and Thursday from 9:00am to 10:00pm. Going to both day school and night school allowed me to carry a full academic program and still hold down a variety of jobs every Friday, Saturday, Sunday and Monday to cover costs. I think it all worked because I always enjoyed what I did. I learned to play squash and worked in a squash club. I became a decent skier and took a job at a ski resort in Vermont . . . first, as a member of the ski patrol, but then as an instructor.

I would leave New York on Thursday evening and ski professionally in Vermont until Monday night . . . . and somehow I still found the time to get my homework finished. I did not own a car in those earlier years, so many times I hitched rides from New York to Vermont out in the cold.

When I graduated from college I took a year off to live in Vermont and ski full time. Recently I did an interview with a major magazine and was quoted as saying: "When I lived in Vermont and skied professionally I earned $85.00 a week and was always broke. Now I earn $1 million a year, don't have time to ski anymore, and I'm still broke . . . What's wrong with this picture?"

My more formal business career started in the early 1960's when I left Vermont to join American Airlines as a management trainee. There I moved through eight promotions in eight years ranging from airport operations to field sales management to general office marketing director. In 1974 I joined a division of Midland Bank as a Vice President. Over the next five years I received five promotions, reaching the position of Executive Vice President and running a $300 million profit center.

I have often been asked how I achieved 13 corporate promotions in 13 years. The answer is actually quite simple: the day I received a promotion I started working on my next. The key to moving ahead in corporate America is to know how to do the job you *want* as well as the person currently holding that job and having senior management know it. When the job opens (and they always do) your boss will evaluate all the candidates and if you are the most capable, chances are you will get it. If you don't, you need to know more about office politics and that's in another book!

I will give you one example of how this worked for me. When I was the Ramp/Ticket Lift Manager for American Airlines at LaGuardia Airport, I wanted to move into sales in the New York region. I felt that having both an operations and a sales background would be best for my career, so I contacted a sales rep and offered to come in on one of my midweek days off to make joint sales calls on his corporate travel managers. I usually worked weekends at the airport and took Monday and Tuesdays off. The rep immediately responded to this as it gave him another great reason to visit his accounts. Having a contact at the airport was important to his corporate travel people since I could V.I.P. their officers, help them when flights were sold out, and smooth things over during bad weather.

For the next three months I made joint calls on one of my days off with almost every sales rep in the New York region. Sure enough, an opening occurred in the region and the district sales manager asked his staff for replacement suggestions. The entire staff told him "Capozzi knows the job, the customers, and the staff better than anyone". With almost 50 candidates, I was offered the job.

The day I started this job I also started working on my next promotion which was to become the National Sales Manager at American's Hotel Division which was then called Americana Hotels. I used the exact same approach and was promoted in less than a year. All in all, this technique earned me my 13 promotions over the next 13 years . . . and it can work for anyone.

In 1979, I was an Executive Vice President for a division of Midland Bank. It was the year my son was born. We had 900 offices in 143 countries and I was traveling about 20 days each month all around the world. I did not want my son to grow up not knowing his father, so in 1979 I decided to quit a great job. I did not know what I was going to do, but I had brought in almost $100 million in new business for my company, so I had the confidence I could earn at least $100,000 going on my own.

I started my current investment banking business in 1979 in the basement of our brownstone in New York City. Over the course of the next two years I formed a variety of companies such as an exposition company that ran shows at the New York Coliseum, a construction company that renovated and sold brownstones in New York City, a consulting company that did work for the United Nations, the Ford Foundation and others, and a management recruitment company with a half dozen Fortune 500 clients.

In 1981, my wife had her second bout with cancer. Memorial Sloan Kettering Hospital gave her six months to live. My daughter had just been born, my son was now two years old, and we were devastated. We decided to sell our home and our business and move to Connecticut with our children to live a simpler life. After liquidating everything, we ended up with a few million dollars and I did not work for the next few years. Somehow my wife survived her bout with cancer, and I had learned that quality of life and family were very important issues to me. I had become the world's best gardener, an expert at doing the laundry, knew all the checkers at the supermarket by their first name, was known as "Mr. Mom" by the kids at school, and had not worn a tie in three years. By 1983 I was really ready to go back to work so I started my investment banking business again. My primary activity was raising capital for start up ventures. I took both a personal equity position in almost every business I funded, and an active role in the marketing of most of them. I have always followed a simple plan: first identify wants and needs in a particular market, develop a marketing plan to solve those wants and needs, provide the capital to start a business to execute the solution, bring in the right people to manage the business, and then sell the business once it is established. If you can indeed get a business that works off the ground, you can always find a buyer. I have started and sold food companies, alarm and security companies, marketing companies, investment companies, and even a communication company. I really don't think it matters what kind of business you start, the key is to identify specific customer "wants and needs" and find a way to provide a solution. Once you have found it, you have accomplished the first (and most important) step in building a business. I call it a "sound business proposition." From it everything else flows.

Another thing I have learned is that, when starting a business, it is best to form "virtual corporations" if you can. These are entities that require a minimal amount of operating capital and rely primarily on the resources of others. For example, I recently started a food company.

The "wants and needs" within the market were for snacks that were fat free . . . but tasted good. Normally with "Better for you foods" the box tastes better than the product. I felt if I could find a way to make fat free taste good, we could build a good business. My wife's background was food. She grew up in the restaurant business, is a French trained chef, and held senior positions in American Airlines' food division.

I asked her to see if she could create formulas for fat free snacks that tasted good. I recruited a group of the foremost scientists in the field to work with her, and after months of work she created a line of great tasting fat free brownies and cookies.

I then invested $500,000 and formed the Greenfield Healthy Foods Company. I explored a variety of bakeries and contracted with one of the largest and finest companies in the baking industry to produce our products. I hired a group of young executives who had experience in food, distribution, marketing, and finance to run our company. We used independent food distributors to bring our products to grocery stores, and in a few years we were in almost every major market in America. Once the company got started, I raised another $2 million from outside investors to fund it until we achieved positive cash flow. We ended up with a business that had no buildings, no factories, no equipment, no trucks, no drivers . . . and very little overhead. We even farmed out all of our accounts receivable and accounts payable. We had created the quintessential "virtual corporation". Our business plan identified that if we were successful in our marketing efforts, we should try to sell our business in five years because it would take the competition about that long to figure out what we were doing and copy us. So, almost five years to the day, we sold our company to the Campbell Soup Company for millions of dollars . . . and sure enough, within a year of our sale there were eight major food companies in the market with fat free brownies and cookies that tasted good. I can honestly say, however, that none ever tasted as good as ours.

Since 1979, I have started 16 companies and have never had a failure. I have helped at least a dozen of my employees become millionaires and I have made a lot of money for my family. On a very personal note, I would like to add to my belief that along with the obvious advantages success in business brings, come important obligations. One of those obligations is to put back at least some of what we have taken out and do our part to insure the future growth of our business community. That future is directly and proportionately related to the quality of the education we provide our children. Our country is rapidly moving away from its roots as a manufacturing and industrial society. Business is becoming increasingly technology-reliant and much less restricted by geographical boundaries each year. Workers must become literate in math, computer science, economics and general business skills to even survive in an entry level position in today's aggressive, competitive and profit conscious business community.

The deterioration of the educational system in America, mainly as a result of budget cuts and particularly in our elementary schools, is of great concern. The growth in social problems (such as welfare) is directly linked to the decreasing quality of our education system. Of even greater concern, we now know we have lost the window of motivation for many of our children before they even graduate from high school.

In addition to the vast reductions in quality education, consider that twenty years ago most children in grades K-12 could not find a place to buy drugs, even if they wanted to. Fifteen years ago most children never considered suicide, regardless of the severity of their depression. Ten years ago many mothers were not forced back to work due to economic uncertainty, and at least one parent was always there to prepare dinner and establish a secure home environment with strong family values.

The twentieth century has brought with it changes in attitudes, and motivation, and significant reductions in ethics and moral values that responsible business leaders must react to. The popular focus of those executives with insight has historically been the support of children at the college level. It is now clear that today our support must be directed to children at a much earlier age, particularly our high risk inner city children who are struggling under depressed economic conditions, pressure to try drugs, rampant criminal dangers, single parent environments, and a significant decline in moral and religious values.

Success in business brings a responsibility to give our children at least the same chance to succeed that we had growing up.

About ten years ago my friend, Ray Chambers, the Founder and Chairman of Wesray, made a great impact on me. Ray is one of the largest supporters of high risk children I know and he opened my eyes to the need for the business community to support education. I joined the Board of one of the most prestigious independent schools in New England

and currently work very hard to raise funding for a variety of scholarship funds for high risk children. As I write this foreword I have taken a position on the organizing committee of the presidents summit for Americas future. It is being chaired by General Colin Powell and I am honored to assist. Our primary mission is to assist children in need.

I hope you enjoy the maxims I have created and collected in this book, and I hope they spark something within you that allows you to move ahead and be successful in your business career.

If this book helps you focus on being more successful in business, I hope it also motivates you to take an active role in some program to help educate our children, and in particular, our high risk children. They represent the future of our business community.

I wish to particularly thank those executives who shared a small measure of their wisdom with me in this book, my wife for putting up with my endless business activities, my children for having what they call "an eccentric Dad", and my mother, father and sister for getting me this far.

I believe if anyone in business reflects on the 500 maxims, anecdotes and stories, contained in this book, they will do better in life ... achieve greater financial success, have stronger bonds with their fellow employees, maintain a higher relationship level with their spouse, and just have more fun. Don't just breeze through each item. Stop for a moment and try to reflect on the meaning or moral.

1.

God gave us two ends: one to sit on and the other to think with. Success depends on which end we use the most.

2.

Your competence level is directly related to your confidence level.

3.

Smart executives know that they do the things they need to do when they need to do them so someday they can do the things they want to do when they want to do them.

4.

Find a job you really enjoy and you'll add five days to every week of your life.

5.

Consider customer complaints as opportunities. At least you can try to salvage these customers . . . but what about the ones who don't complain and just go away?

6.
You Are Known By The Friends You Keep

In 1974 I submitted a membership application for a very close Jewish friend at my very prestigious athletic club located in Manhattan. Subsequently, I was contacted by a member of the Admissions Committee who asked me to withdraw my application because "we don't want Jewish members." I couldn't believe my ears, immediately handed him my membership card, and have never been back since. In my business career, I have found that I always do better when I don't compromise my values. To this day my friend is still my friend and, guess what, I found another club to join that didn't make me feel uncomfortable.

7.
An executive who thinks the customer isn't important should try doing without him for an operating quarter.

8.
If you want to get ahead at work, do your job as if you owned the business.

9

If You Haven't Learned How To Not Do Things, Don't Learn

Peter Rogers is an investor in several of my companies and sits on a variety of my Boards. He has been the President or Chairman of many very successful companies, including Nabisco. He's also one of the brightest marketing people I have ever met and while he doesn't have an MBA, he does have a B.S. and a Ph.D. He sent me the following story which I would like to share with you.

"In the mid 1980's, when I was appointed President of Nabisco Brands USA,—a $6 billion group of businesses comprised of companies such as Del Monte, The Nabisco Biscuit Company, Nabisco Foods, Planters Peanut Company, Lifesavers, and others. I was asked a very simple question, "How on earth did you get to be where you are without having an MBA???"

"My response was "because I was never taught how not to do things. I practice the art of the possible." What I meant by this was really a modest condemnation of the typical MBA curriculum of the 1960's through the early 1980's. In those days, most MBA candidates were taught by the case study method. A technique based on analysis, most of which was numerical. This method of teaching, coupled with early life experiences in multiple-choice examination methods, leads students to study those aspects of a business that can be quantified and are amenable to numerical analysis. Non-tangible aspects such as timing, judgment, leadership and just "plain luck" are often not subject to critical scrutiny, and yet these are often the most critical "keys to success" in a business. Practicing the art of the possible, putting reasonable reliance on intuition, judgment and "accumulated wisdom" is often a necessary counter-balance to pure analytical analysis of the quantifiable aspects of a business situation. Thus it is not always necessary to have an MBA in order to be able to lead, excite, motivate and discipline."

10.

"Nearly every man who develops an idea, works it up to the point where it looks impossible, and then gets discouraged. That's not the place to become discouraged."

—Thomas Edison

11.

All executives make less mistakes when their mouths are shut.

12.

<u>There Is Always A Right Way And A Wrong Way</u>
<u>To Succeed</u>

Two Jesuit priests both wanted a cigarette while they prayed. They decided to ask their bishop for permission. The first asked but was told no. A little while later he spotted his friend smoking. "Why did the Bishop allow you to smoke and not me?", he asked. "Because you asked if you could smoke while you prayed and I asked if I could pray while I smoked!" the friend replied.

13.

You know you're working too hard when the night cleaning lady invites you to her daughter's wedding.

14.

"One difference in working for yourself is the level of your goals. When you work for yourself, you set high goals and try to exceed them. When you work for someone else you set lower goals and try to achieve them."

—Eric Klar

15.

The difference between an experienced businessman and an educated businessman is that an
educated businessman recognizes his mistakes and
then makes them again.

16.

Age is a function of mind over matter and if you don't
mind . . . it doesn't matter.

17.

No executive can value the worth of others unless he
first learns to value himself.

18.

Wealth comes to those who make things happen; not
to those who let things happen.

19.
Always Maintain A Positive Attitude

Many years ago a large American shoe manufacturer sent two sales reps out to different parts of the
Australian outback to see if they could drum up some
business among the aborigines. Some time later the
company received telegrams from both agents. The
first one said, "No business here . . . natives don't

wear shoes." The second one said, "Great opportunity here . . . natives don't wear shoes!"

20.

Success is getting what you want; happiness is wanting what you get.

21.

Only a fool tries to build his reputation on the things he plans to do.

22.

Any businessman who has ever failed at something should remember that even in baseball you can strike out two of three times at bat and still make a million dollars a year.

23.

Problems that appear to be easy to solve always belong to someone else.

24.

Never slow dance with your boss's spouse at the annual Christmas party.

25.

In Business Don't Worry About How You Look . . .
Worry About How You Act

Historically, world leaders who are remembered for their accomplishments, are rarely remembered for their appearance . . . or lack thereof. Most have been rather common looking. Consider Abraham Lincoln. He attended a party one night and overheard a rather stuffy woman comment on his appearance: "He's a very common-looking man." Lincoln responded: "The Lord prefers common-looking people. That is why he makes so many of them."

26.

The executive who works from 8:00 a.m. to 8:00 p.m. every day will be both very successful and fondly remembered by his widow's next husband.

Those Who Succeed In Business Know Their Limits And Know How To Go Beyond Those Limits

In 1996, the famous photographer, Annie Leibowitz, published a wonderful study of Olympic portraits. In an interview on the Today Show she described sprinter Dennis Mitchell as "so fast that when I developed my film he wasn't there!" Annie then moved her lens further forward so that Mitchell and the shutter arrived in the same place at the same time and she captured an absolutely amazing shot of the world class sprinter.

28.

Speak when you're angry and you'll make the best speech you'll ever regret.

29.

Executives who want their employees to have their feet on the ground must first put some responsibility on their shoulders.

Do Your Work At Work

Many business people have unsuccessful marriages or poor relationships with their children because they never learned to do their work at work.

In business, if we want to win, we plan carefully, execute properly, and follow up on a very timely basis. To have a successful relationship with your spouse or children, you must also plan, execute and follow up with the same degree of effort as you do in your corporate life.

What would your boss think about you if you missed every important function? Why should your kids hold you in high regard if you miss all of their games or school functions? Do you think you would get the next promotion if you arrive late for every company meeting? Why should your spouse feel great about you if you are never home on time?

Not long ago, Christopher A. Sinclair, head of the $11 billion worldwide Pepsico, Inc. beverage operation, resigned after 14 years of service. In his statement he was quoted: "The intensity of the challenge and the frequency of travel have exacted a price on my family and has led me to reassess my priorities."

John Cleese is credited with the story of a man

doing paperwork in bed late into the evening. Trying to sleep, his very aggravated wife finally challenges him to turn off the light and go to sleep. He explains that he can't because he must finish his work. She asks the key question: "Why don't you do your work at work?" His reply: "I can't, I am at meetings all day." Now, really curious, she questions: "Well, when do you sleep?" His reply: "I sleep in meetings like everyone else!"

Try to avoid distractions or unproductive meetings that drain your time if you really want to succeed. The truly successful businessperson learns how to get his or her work done at work.

31.

If you smell horse crap when you enter the barn, look around and you'll probably find a horse's ass. The same is true in most board meetings.

32.
Don't Blame The Tomatoes

If a gardener plants tomatoes and they don't grow, the smart gardener doesn't blame the tomatoes but immediately investigates the source of the problem . . . not enough sun; needs more water; may need fertilizer.

When a business isn't growing, the smart executive shouldn't fire his employees but investigate the source of the problem . . . competition; pricing; quality; distribution; etc. Once management knows what's wrong, solutions can be attempted.

33.

In Business, As In Life, If You Fall Down Get Up And Keep Going If You Want To Win

Bonny St. John Dean was born with one leg. That never stopped her. She excelled at everything she did, including getting a job in the White House. She even learned to ski with one leg. She became so good that she participated in the 1984 Para-Olympics in Innsbrook, Austria. During the race she fell, but immediately got up and kept going. She took third and won a Bronze Medal. When told that the Gold Medal winner also fell on the course, she commented that if you fall down, you can still win the Gold . . . Just be sure to get up faster!

34.

Very Few Of Us Never Make Mistakes

During a fiery exchange at a summit meeting between President Kennedy and Premier Kruschev, Kennedy asked the Russian Premier: "Do you ever admit a mistake?"

"Certainly I do," Kruschev responded. "In a speech before the 20th Party Congress I admitted all of Stalin's mistakes." To be successful in business you must recognize your mistakes . . . if only not to make them again.

35.

"You may have achieved price and selection parity . . . but the experts say . . . and our customers confirm . . . Customer Service is the next battleground in retailing."

—Dale C. Pond

Senior Vice President, Marketing

Lowe's

36.

The best way to appreciate your job is to be without it for awhile.

37.

"It's the law of the universe that the strong shall survive and the weak must fall by the way, and I don't care what idealistic plan is cooked up, nothing can change that."

—Walt Disney

38.

Fortunately, an employee's mind, once stretched by creative thinking never regains its original size.

39.

"Genius is one percent inspiration and ninety-nine percent perspiration."

—Thomas Edison

40.

When the going gets easy, it's time for a reality check . . . you might be going downhill.

41.

In all my years in business, I have found that people in meetings tend to agree on decisions that, as individuals, they know are dumb.

42.
<u>A Sign Of The Times</u>

As a boy I started my first job at age 10, selling soda at a construction site. At 14 I set pins at a manual bowling alley, sold hot dogs at 15, and worked in construction at 16. I couldn't wait for "snow days." Not because I didn't have to go to school, but because I could shovel snow from 6:00am to 8:00pm and make what was then a fortune.

To teach my 16 year old son work ethics, I had him working every summer, but one day I asked him to help me build a shed behind my barn. I told him that someday he would have his own place and he would need to know how to build things. His response was: " I'm not going to do that. I am going to earn a lot of money and hire someone to do that!"

43.
We do not stop working because we are old; we grow old because we stop working.

44.
The smart executive is the one who knows what he should do . . . the smarter executive is the one who knows what he shouldn't do.

45.

An executive's greatest reward for success is not what he's paid for it but what he becomes because of it.

46.

Successful Leadership Depends On One's Ability To Make People Want To Follow Rather Than Have To Follow

General Eisenhower used to demonstrate the art of leadership with a simple piece of string. He'd put it on a table and say: "Pull it and it'll follow wherever you wish. Push it and it will go nowhere." Managers who prod rather than lead rarely obtain the maximum performance from their employees.

47.

You'll learn more about a road by traveling it than by consulting all the maps in the world.

48.

The first step you should take if you want to be successful is to decide what kind of executive you are. Executives fall into three categories: Those who make things happen; those who watch things happen; and those who wonder what happened.

49.

In business people take different roads to achieve success. Just because they're not on your road doesn't mean they've gotten lost.

50.

Employees are like children. Don't expect them to listen to your advice and to ignore your example.

51.

The difference between an employee that says "Let me do that for you" and one that says "That's not my job" is that the latter should be working for your biggest competitor.

52.

"Follow up is the Chariot of Genius"

—Terry Lierman
President Capital Associates, Inc.
Washington, DC

53.

Long Term Success Is A Result Of A Series Of Short Term Successes

As I write this book I can't help thinking about many of the people that have contributed to its content. It will be interesting to look back in ten or twenty years to see how many have moved up the corporate ladder. The above maxim was sent to me by Steven S. Reinemund, Chairman and CEO, Frito-Lay Company. Years ago, Steve had stayed overnight in our home and I can remember discussing business, kids, and life in general in my kitchen over Belgian Waffles. What struck me most was his tremendous value system and integrity . . . even more than his professionalism in business. Steve is someone that will continue to move up the corporate ladder and in his case I really believe "up" is totally undefinable. If you invest in any company that is run by Steve Reinemund . . . you will not lose. His above maxim about long term success is so correct and so very "Reinemund."

54.

People who wait for all conditions to be perfect before acting, never act.

55.

"I would rather lose in a cause that will someday win, than win in a cause that will someday lose."

—Woodrow Wilson

56.

Don't be in a hurry to become successful, you might just rush right past it.

57.

Answer The Need, Not Just The Question

My friend, Jack Kliger, who is the Executive Vice President for Conde Nast Publications and manages one of the largest publishing entities in the world still finds the time to be involved in substantial community service work. A great role model for all of us. He is also an investor in many of my companies. He shared the following with me not long ago:

"When I was being trained as a sales rep, an old pro took me out to "show me the ropes." He first stopped into a candy store and asked the proprietor for a flint for his cigarette lighter. The owner said he didn't carry them; we turned around and left. As soon as we got out, the old pro looked at me and asked: "What did he do wrong?" I said I didn't know. The pro said: "He didn't try to sell me matches!"

58.

If your only choice is to hire either a conceited executive or a foolish executive, hire the conceited one . . . occasionally he won't be conceited.

59.

Sometimes the things we get for nothing end up costing us the most.

60.
Tomorrows Are What Counts

Many executives continue to look to the past as a planning guide for the future. However, given the explosive growth we are experiencing in technology and its huge impact on business, today's executives must look to the future to plan for the future.

I have done business with Merrill Lynch & Company for many years and Dave Komansky, their CEO, recently gave me the following which I totally endorse for anyone reading this book:

"Looking over our shoulders and enjoying past results doesn't mean a damn thing. Tomorrow's are what count. I am not a yesterday person. If we did well yesterday that is history. What I am worried about is how we are going to perform five years from now."

Executives like Dave Komansky who are always looking forward are far less likely to be surprised by their competition . . . quite the contrary, I am sure the competition asks "What's Merrill Lynch doing today."

61.

The best time to save some money is when you have some.

62.

Be careful. Sometimes when you poke a snake it will bite you.

63.

"Everything should be made as simple as possible, but not simpler."

—Albert Einstein

64.

Hire Employees With Different Strengths

I've started a lot of businesses and have learned that we all have a natural tendency to surround ourselves with employees who think and act the same way we do. We instinctively want everyone to be our friends. This isn't always the best policy for building a business. Try to hire the most effective staff. Build a complementary team in which your employees' strengths complement your weaknesses.

65.

A fat lawsuit is never as smart as a lean compromise.

66.

"Most folks are about as happy as they make up their minds to be."

—Abraham Lincoln

67.

"Good people don't exist well in a bad environment"

—Sue Galati
Vice President, Sales
Relationship Marketing Group

68.
Success Requires Focus

Charlie McCarthy, Chief Operating Officer, Tetley USA, Inc., is about the best Operations Executive I have ever met and he has a wonderful way with people. Because he has been President of Campbell Soup Sales Company and President of Pepperidge Farm, and is also an owner and Board member in one of my companies, I have a great deal of respect for Charlie's advice. Over dinner one night he told me the following:

"In business our challenge is to put all of our activities into one of three buckets. The first contains those things that add value to our lives and our companies. The second contains activities that keep our business steady and orderly. And third is for all those other things that everybody asks you to do. Successful leaders spend most of their time working on Bucket # One. I also call it focus!"

69.

It isn't the employees you terminate who make your life miserable, it's the ones you don't.

70.
A Positive Attitude Is Critical For Success

Throughout this book I will continuously reference my belief in the value of a positive attitude for success. I recently received a wonderful maxim from Jack MacDonough, the Chairman and Chief Operating Officer at Miller Brewing Company that is so very correct on the subject that I wanted to share it with you.

Jack said:

"Things work out best for people who make the best of the way things work out."

71.

We are continually faced by great opportunities brilliantly disguised as insoluble problems.

72.

The best way to convince a foolish executive he is wrong is to let him have his way.

73.

The low bidder is usually someone who is wondering what he left out.

74.

Almost no quality products sell for a cheap price.

75.

"The true test of our progress is not whether we add more to the abundance of those who have too much; it is whether we provide enough for those who have too little."

—Franklin D. Roosevelt

76.

Successful executives do not spend valuable time finding faults, they spend time finding remedies.

Our Business Furture Begins With Investing In Our Children's Future

For over a year, I have watched John assemble items of wisdom pertaining to success in business for his book and wanted to contribute the above maxim since it is the philosophy which drives my work both inside and outside of Harpo.

I strongly believe that it is in the best interest of every business executive to think critically about our impact on the next generation. This philosophy is driven by economics, as well as social goals. If we don't take care of our children today, we will all pay a price tommorow in both terror and taxes. Our children who are at risk of child abuse and neglect are only at one end of this continuum. At the other end is the potential to provide all chlidren with optimal environments in which they grow and thrive, investing in the next generation of leaders, thinkers, voters and consumers.

To put this theory into action, the Harpo Entertainment Group has maintained a commitment to providing quality television and film production which educates the public about issues which are important to all of us as citizens. I created the non-profit organization CIVITAS as the logical next step in giving back to our nation's children.

The mission of CIVITAS, a latin word meaning "return to community" is to discover and communicate real-world solutions to problems impeding the optimal development of children. To this end, it partners with and private insitutions to support innovations in any area that will have a systemic impact on the health and welfare of children. In the near future, we will create a communications and media component of CIVITAS Initiative which will rapidly disseminate "what works" to policy makers and the public.

The net/net of these efforts is clear, since true success in business requires more than short term thinking, and short term profits. Investing in the healthy, development of children will catalyze positive change in our businesses and our communities, yielding a return exponentially larger than what we currently believe is possible.

—Jeffrey D. Jacobs
Founder, CIVITAS Initiative
President, Harpo Entertainment Group

78.

Experienced business travelers know that motel mattresses are better on the side away from the phone.

79.

If you are in business and have intelligence you don't need to have much else; if you don't have intelligence, it doesn't matter what else you have.

80.

Great leadership is the ability to get employees to do what they don't want to do and like doing it.

81.

Creditors always seem to have much better memories than debtors.

82.

Executives who speak with more claret than clarity usually end up speaking to themselves.

83.

What Goes Around Comes Around

In 1872 George Westinghouse, the famous inventor, received his first patent for an automatic air brake that worked far better than the brakes currently being used on trains. He wrote to Cornelius Vanderbilt, President of the New York Central Railroad, identifying the advantages of his new invention. Vanderbilt returned his letter but wrote across the bottom: "I have no time to waste on fools."

Westinghouse then approached the Pennsylvania Railroad who immediately became interested in his invention and funded further development. News of the success of the air brake reached Vanderbilt who wrote Westinghouse a letter asking him to set up a meeting. Westinghouse sent the letter back to Vanderbilt with the notation, "I have no time to waste on fools," scrawled across the bottom.

Vanderbilt eventually purchased Air Brakes from Westinghouse at a greatly increased price.

84.

To improve in business, listen carefully to all your enemies . . . They are the ones that will bluntly point out your faults.

85.

There is no limit to what you can achieve if you don't mind who gets the credit.

86.

One of God's greatest miracles is to enable ordinary people to do extraordinary things.

87.
Really, What Is Failure?

Most inventors tell you they try about 999 times to make an invention work. Once it does, they do very well. The successful inventor treats his failures simply as practice shots.

88.

Worry about little expenses. Remember a small leak will ultimately sink any great ship.

89.

Not deciding is deciding to do nothing.

90.

The successful executive never allows his employees to complain about a problem unless they offer an idea about a solution.

91.

Image Is Important

At a New York party Mohammed Ali, the world heavyweight boxing champion, was introduced to violinist Isaac Stern. Stern remarked: "You might say we're in the same business . . . we both earn a living with our hands." Ali replied: "You must be pretty good; there isn't a mark on you."

92.

Better to ask twice than to lose your way once.

93.

In business, as in forest fires, big problems always start out small.

94.

Successful executives learn to forgive and forget their enemies . . . They also keep a record of their names.

95.

"Always swing hard, in case you happen to hit the ball."

—Duke Snider

96.

In business it's nice to be important, but to be respected it's important to be nice.

97.

At The Core Of Every Big Problem Is A Simple Solution

A number of years ago, when I was just starting out in business, I was fortunate to have a friend who taught me how to reduce very complex situations to simple ones. His lesson involved stepping back and not getting caught up in tons of detail. One such lesson involved analyzing a business that was losing money. This business had seven operating divisions. My mentor asked his Chief Financial Officer to spread out the P & L's for each division on the Board Room table. The first thing he did was to pick up the four P & L's that were in the black. He then told the CFO that if we simply removed the three divisions that were losing money, all we would have left were those divisions that were making money . . . problem solved. After all was said and done, he did get rid of two of the divisions and brought the third into the black.

98.

Don't ever think about how good you are, think about how great you can be.

99.
Follow The Simple Fork On The Road To Success

Thomas Edison was very skilled in hiring executives, particularly when hiring engineers. In one unique test, he would give an applicant an empty bulb and ask: "How much water will it hold?"

Obviously there were two ways to find the answer. One way was to utilize your skill as an engineer and via the use of special gauges, measure the surface area of the bulb and then convert this data to identify volume. This could take almost 30 minutes to accomplish.

The other method was to simply fill the bulb with water and pour the contents into a standard measuring cup. Time to accomplish this feat? . . .About 30 seconds.

Engineers who utilized their skills by the first route were thanked politely and dismissed. Those who chose the simple route were hired.

100.
Leave your work at your office or you'll leave your marriage at your lawyer's.

101.
Always make the most of the best and the least of the worst.

102.
"The Height Of Your Altitude Will Be Determined By Your Attitude Not Your Aptitude"

A number of years ago, I had the pleasure of doing business with Gary L. Harrison who runs the specialty baking group for Flowers Industries, a multi billion dollar food company that owns Keebler, Mrs. Smith's and many others.

Gary and I have become good friends and I have always admired his attitude and judgment in business. One story in particular that comes to mind is his philosophy about co-packing. He will bake products for anyone . . . even his biggest competitors. He feels it's more important to get the maximum utilization possible out of his plant, people and equipment than it is to worry about his competitors being in the market with him.

I will always remember his comment:

"Hell, if I don't make products for them, they'll just go someplace else, and if I can't stop them from competing with me I might as well make something on the production side."

Gary will always be successful in business because he has a winning attitude, and a clarity of direction that all highly successful executives require. He sent me the above maxim and I know its one reason he is so successful.

103.

Try Not To Argue With Someone
Smarter Than You

As a young man Winston Churchill sported a mustache. At a political dinner he got into an argument with an older woman who, attempting to put him down, commented: "Mr. Churchill, I care for neither your politics nor your mustache." "Madam", responded Churchill, "you are quite unlikely to come into contact with either."

104.

An executive who swears he's never made a mistake, works for a boss who made a big one.

105.

"If a man is called to be a street sweeper, he should sweep streets even as Michaelangelo painted, or Beethoven composed music, or Shakespeare wrote poetry. He should sweep streets so well that all the hosts of heaven and earth will pause to say, here lived a great street sweeper who did his job well.

—Martin Luther King, Jr.

Remember, you spend at least eight hours of your day with your secretary and only about three hours a day with your wife . . . and your wife knows it. Send a gift once in a while for no reason at all . . . to your wife.

107.
There's No Such Thing As A Stupid Idea

Along the way in my business career, I have met some wonderful and stimulating people that I really enjoy working with. One such person is Ted Giannitti, Jr., the Chief Financial Officer at Greenfield . . . a company I started and ultimately sold to the Campbell Soup Company. Ted gave me his thoughts on brainstorming which I hope you agree with:

"I worked for someone earlier in my career that practiced the concept:" There's no such thing as a stupid idea." In meetings our entire staff would be encouraged to suggest anything that came to mind that would improve our business. The first time someone laughed at a suggestion, the boss asked him to leave the meeting. From that point on, we all knew it was okay to suggest anything without intimidation. I witnessed some of the stupidest ideas begin to develop into magnificent "out of the box" concepts. People got excited and statements like "great . . . but what if we added this or did that . . . followed. Positive feedback generates new ideas, stimulates creative expression, and allows every employee to actually participate in all levels of business.

108.
Mushroom Management

If you leave your employees in the dark, constantly give them lots of horse crap, and let them hibernate unattended for awhile, you'll have employees who are more like mushrooms than productive workers . . . and the best thing they can then hope for is to be canned.

109.
When considering a new supervisor for your shipping department, give him an open road map and see if he can fold it up again.

110.
The problem with success is that by the time you're rich enough to sleep late, you're so old you always wake up early.

111.

The greatest tragedy in business is not that you tried and failed, but that you failed to try.

112.

He Who Laughs First Doesn't Always Laugh Last

George Bernard Shaw, the famous playwright, sent Winston Churchill two tickets to the opening of his play, Saint Joan, with a note: "One for yourself and one for a friend—if you have one." Churchill replied that he regretted being unable to attend the opening, but asked if it would be possible to have tickets for the second night—"If there is one."

113.

Winning executives see an answer for every problem. Losing executives see a problem for every answer.

114.

"The journey of a thousand miles starts with a single step."

—Chinese proverb

115.

There is very little difference in most executives . . . but that little difference makes a very big difference. The little difference is attitude. The big difference is whether it is positive or negative.

116.

Try not to argue with someone when he is right.

117.

"If you go into a battle, it's better to win the first time."

—General George S. Patton

118.

"I count him braver who overcomes his desires than him who conquers his enemies; for the hardest victory is the victory over self."

—Aristotle

119.

Some executives dream of becoming wealthy while others stay awake and achieve it.

120.

If you study the statistics, you'll find that generous people have far fewer emotional problems.

121.

Some People Are Lucky And Some Are Not

John Paul Getty, the oil executive and billionaire, once received a request from a magazine for a short article that explained his great success. The billionaire obligingly wrote: "Some people find oil—others don't".

122.

When weighing the faults of others, be careful not to put your thumb on the scale.

123.

One difference between most successful executives and most unsuccessful ones is that with unsuccessful executives, when all is said and done, more is said than done.

124.

"There are two types of employees: Those who do the work and those who take the credit. Try to be in the first group; there is much less competition there."

—Indira Gandhi

125.

Job security is being worth more than you're getting paid.

126.

When interviewing a new candidate, ask yourself how you'd feel if the person were working for your largest competitor rather than you.

127.

The very smart executive is smarter than most other people, and smart enough to not tell them so.

128.

It is easier to accept difficult people if you recognize that most of them feel so small inside that they need to act big and obnoxious outside.

129.

"Practice does not make perfect. Only perfect practice makes perfect."

—Vince Lombardi-Former NFL Coach

130.

Enemies can indeed come back to haunt you. Sometimes it just takes a little time.

131.

"Nobody ever got into trouble by keepin' his mouth shut."

—Forrest Gump

132.

"It takes years to build a reputation for integrity but it only takes a poor decision and a brief moment to lose it forever."

—Richard R. Fogarty
Former Chairman and CEO
Labatt USA

133.

"Don't accept your dog's admiration as conclusive evidence that you are wonderful."

—Ann Landers

134.

"I know it's wrong, but every once in a while, if you really get mad, it's okay to just stomp that sucker flat."

—Lyndon Baines Johnson

135.

"See nothing less than perfection because, even though that in itself might be an impossible goal, you will discover great things during the pursuit."

—Steven Wardell

136.

If there are things about a job candidate you don't like, you will like them even less after you hire him.

137.

Learn from the mistakes of others. You won't live long enough to make them all yourself.

138.

Respect people for who they are, not what you want them to be.

139.

If you play golf with your boss and win he'll want to play again. If he doesn't, he'll probably fire you and it doesn't matter.

140.

It always takes more effort to figure out what's right than what's wrong . . . but the extra effort is always worth it.

141.

Sometimes when you're holding a 900 lb. gorilla by the ankle it's best to let him run away.

142.
Sometimes It's Best To Just Mind Your Own Business

At a political dinner party a slightly intoxicated Winston Churchill became engaged in a heated exchange with a female member of Parliament. At the end of the exchange the lady scornfully remarked, "Mr. Churchill, you are drunk." Churchill replied: "And you, Madame, are ugly . . . but tomorrow I shall be sober."

143.
If you think education is expensive, wait till you see what ignorance costs you.

144.
Avoid shortcuts. They always take too much time in the long run.

145.
Executive personalities can sometime be measured by their actions. For example, in driving, there are two types of executive motorists—those who drive as if they owned the road, and those who drive as if they owned the car.

146.

When You Think Things Can't Get Worse, There's Always Tomorrow

John Mariucci, when coaching the U.S. Olympic Hockey team, became impatient with his young and inexperienced team. During one particular low moment he screamed: "Every day you guys look worse and worse . . . today you played like tomorrow."

147.
Those who fail to prepare are always prepared to fail.

148.
Don't envy executives who have everything . . . most of them haven't paid for it yet.

149.
Tell an employee something about someone else only if you don't mind someone else finding out.

150.
People who don't work with great enthusiasm are a danger to the entire business and should be fired with great enthusiasm.

151.

"You can't score if you keep the bat on your shoulder."

—Casey Stengel

152.

The greatest mistake an executive can make is to be afraid of making a mistake.

153.

"The devil hath power to assume a pleasing shape."

—William Shakespeare

154.

"One machine can do the work of 100 ordinary men. No machine can do the work of one extraordinary man."

—Henry Ford

155.

Reacting is much easier than thinking and failing is much easier than success.

156.

Knowledge becomes wisdom only after it has been put to good use.

157.
Analyze The Facts Before Making Key Decisions

On June 25, 1876, General George Armstrong
Custer received information that a significant num-
ber of Indians were gathering at the Little Big Horn.
Without analyzing the facts, he decided to ride out
with 250 men to "surround" almost 3,000 Indians.
This was a serious mistake.

158.
Nothing is interesting if you're not interested.

159.
Most of one's unhappiness is the direct result of com-
paring yourself to others.

160.
The issue is not the anger, it's how you express it.

161.
Most executives who must control are actually terri-
fied of losing control.

162.
Frequent praise is always more effective than de-
layed criticism.

163.
Never eat chili before a board meeting.

164.
If you have to downsize, first get rid of those executives that think but never do and then those that do but never think.

165.
<u>Motivate Your Employees To Motivate
Your Business</u>

In almost every business I've started I've given my employees free equity. The difference in attitude and performance is amazing. When times were difficult, the average employee would have quit to find another job. The equity employee hung in there and made it work. I can honestly say that I have made almost a dozen employees millionaires during my business career, which makes me very happy. Even if you can't give your people equity, it's still important to motivate them. Something as simple as giving them an upgraded title or a corner office with a window will make a huge difference . . . to the employee and to your business.

166.

Experienced executives know that the quality of a hotel is directly proportionate to the thickness of the towels.

167.

Jeff McElnea is the President and CEO of Einson Freeman, a promotion agency that was ranked fourth in the top ten agencies by Promo Magazine. Their client list reads like Who's Who in some of the finest companies in America. Jeff gave me his personal view on leadership and I thought I would share it with you:

"A business manager becomes a true leader when he or she can adeptly balance the needs of customers, employees and shareholders, while adding value to all three."

168.

Try not to work for a company that makes or sells anything you wouldn't want to give to your family . . . life is just too short.

169.

Great executives change their jobs for the sake of their principles . . . stupid ones change their principles for the sake of their job.

170.

Perseverance is knocking long enough at the gate to wake someone up.

171.

Ability is one of the most important strengths that any executive needs for success . . . Specifically, the ability to recognize ability in others.

172.

Nothing kills employee morale and productivity faster than a boss who makes every decision. Give your staff the power and authority to grow and so will your business.

173.

The optimist finds opportunity in every difficulty; not difficulty in every opportunity.

174.

In a meeting, never argue with a fool. Your boss may not know which one is which.

175.

Only buy equipment at wholesale that never needs to be fixed.

176.

Never encourage your son to date your boss's daughter.

177.

In business there are two types of employees: those who work as if they are employees, and those who work as if they are employers. When a promotion becomes available, who do you think will get the position?

178.

In business as in history you can always identify the pioneer who takes big risks and moves into new territories . . . he's the one with all the arrows in his back! But we would have never reached new frontiers without them.

179.

The easiest way to knock a chip off someone's shoulder is give them a pat on the back.

180.

Don't brag; it's not the whistle that moves the train.

181.

If you are going to lose your job, be sure it's for what you did . . . not for what you didn't do.

182.

Beware of the most dangerous person in business—- the articulate incompetent.

183.
"Failure Is Only The Opportunity To Begin Again More Intelligently"

The maxim is credited to Henry Ford, but there are so many other successful people that come to mind every time I read it. One of my most favorite heroes is the legendary Colonel Sanders. In 1952, at the age of 62, while in personal bankruptcy, he started the Kentucky Fried Chicken Company in Corbin, Kentucky. While living out of his car, with only a recipe for fried chicken and a $105 a month Social Security check, he began again and went on to build a multi-million dollar food company.

184.

It doesn't matter if your name is on the outside of an office door or on the flap of your shirt pocket . . . everyone is important to the success of a company. The main difference, however, is that the guy with his name on the office door usually costs the company a lot more if he screws up.

185.
The Lord Works In Mysterious Ways

At a recent dinner with a friend who runs a Fortune 500 Company, he told me a story about a man who was voted the least likely to succeed in high school but went on to become a multimillionaire. When asked how he did it he replied: "I produce my products for $1.25 each and sell them for $12.50 each . . . with my 10% mark up I can't help but make lots of money.

Editor's Note: For those of you who took Liberal Arts in school rather than Finance, please read this twice.

186.

To enjoy success, you've got to experience some failure in your life; otherwise you won't appreciate the difference.

187.

A good scare is usually worth more than good advice.

188.

In business it isn't hard to be smart from time to time. It's hard being smart all the time.

189.

Senior executives are really not more mature. They just have more money . . . which makes them appear more mature.

190.

When an executive retires and time is no longer as important, why does his company usually give him a gold watch?

191.

The successful businessman will promise only what he can deliver . . . then deliver more than he promised.

192.

The next time you feel disappointed because you didn't get what you wanted, think about all the things you did get that you didn't want.

193.

If someone is pushing you in an unreasonable fashion, tell him, "You can have it right, or you can have it now. You just can't have it right now!"

194.

Be Loyal To The People Who Deliver For You, Life Has A Habit Of Coming Full Circle

Some people can do anything and do it well. A good friend, Mike Lorelli, was a senior executive at Pepsi, became a President at Pizza Hut, moved on as President of Tambrands and then to MobileComm as their CEO. In between he wrote a great book called Traveling Again Dad which anyone with kids should own if they travel a lot. To his credit, Mike donates the profits of his book to various children's charities. Mike's philosophy about dealing with people is so correct that I thought I would share it with you:

"My former assistant in Wichita recently called me and asked if I would give her a letter of reference. She was a terrific employee and I immediately faxed her a great recommendation. This may seem like a little thing, but I know that if she ever relocated to New York and I needed another highly competent assistant, I could count on her to join me.

Six years ago, when I was running Pizza Hut's International Division, my former Executive Vice President wanted to bounce off a career option on me. I was overseas in Poland at the time. However, I immediately called him back, gave him my thoughts, and he ultimately took a position with another company. We lost touch for a few years but recently I needed a person with his exceptional skills. I called him and based upon our past relationship he has now relocated to join me as a valuable member of my executive staff."

195.
Most happy executives are nice executives. If your boss is not such a nice boss, chances are he isn't very happy either.

196.
Even if you are highly qualified, you must act the part in order to get the part. If you don't act like you can do the job, you probably won't get the job.

197.
"Any man who views the world at 50 the same way he did at 20 has wasted 30 years of his life."

—Mohammed Ali

198.

The next time you are having a bad day, remember that even gray skies are just clouds passing over.

—Teddy Roosevelt

199.

Dumb executives have a talent for saying the correct thing at the proper time to the wrong people.

200.

Executives under sixty usually like gifts that are electronic. Executives over sixty usually like anything alcoholic.

201.
Teamwork Is A Powerful Force

A few years ago, I was riding in a chairlift with my son while skiing in the French Alps. Suddenly, about 100 yards away, an avalanche broke free from the top of the mountain and roared down the slope. It was a frightening experience. On reflection, I thought about how delicate and fragile a single snowflake was, and yet how powerful the force can become when many snowflakes stick together.

202.

Plotting revenge only allows the people who hurt you to hurt you longer.

203.

Sometimes the only way around the mountain is to climb over it.

204.

Business can actually be more dangerous than war. In war you can only be killed once but in business it can happen many times.

205.

When you pay peanuts, you get monkeys.

206.

It takes great skill to make many of your business guests feel at home, even when you wish they were.

207.

The easiest thing to achieve in business with almost no effort is failure . . . but success isn't about "easy" is it?

208.

If you aren't happy with what you've got now, what makes you think you'll be happier with more?

209.

Never volunteer to confront the company president with the demands of all the other employees.

210.

The next time you complain about your problems . . . remember if they weren't so difficult someone with less ability would probably have your job.

211.

Worrying about what's right is always more important than worrying about who's right.

212.

"Too many times . . . too many of us . . . are simply too far removed from the issues to fully assess them. It isn't that we can't find the solution. It's that we can't see the problem."

—Bob Tillman
President, CEO
Lowe's Companies, Inc.

213.

Chief executives discuss concepts. Senior executives discuss events. Middle executives discuss people. Non-executives discuss tasks. As a step in moving ahead in corporate life, step up one level in your discussions.

214.

Usually the person who is the first to jump up and throw another log on the fire is not the one who had to split the wood in the first place.

215.

Don't hold a $1,000 meeting to solve a $100 problem.

216.

The major difference between a successful person and one who isn't is usually a lack of confidence to try.

217.

Problems that affect everyone are best solved by everyone.

218.

To succeed, no matter how silly your ideas may seem, speak up. Remember, the forest would be very silent if no birds sang except the very best.

219.

No one can make you feel inferior without your permission.

220.

"All of our dreams can come true, if we have the courage to pursue them."

—Walt Disney

221.

An executive too busy to take care of his employees is like a mechanic too busy to take care of his tools.

222.

Sometimes money just costs too much.

223.

Lawyers earn more from problems than solutions.

224.

Junior executives get . . . middle executives improve . . . senior executives spend.

225.

Don't be afraid to go out on a limb: that's where the fruit is.

226.

No matter what the issue, no one ever won an argument with a customer.

227.

You never get a second chance to make a first impression.

228.

Business is like riding a bicycle. Either you keep up your speed or you'll fall down.

229.

Don't make difficult people the center of your emotional life.

230.

Profit projections are sometimes similar to the horizon which is defined as an imaginary line that disappears as you get closer.

231.

God gave us two ears and one mouth so we could listen twice as much as we talk.

232.

Try not to work for a person who has more problems than you do.

233.

Keeping up is always easier than catching up.

234.

All Successful Business Builders Learn To Think Outside The Box

Mark H. McCormack, the Founder of International Management Group, once wrote:

"Business demands innovation. There is a constant need to feel around the fringes, to test the edges, but business schools, out of necessity are condemned to teach the past. This not only perpetuates conventional thinking; it stifles innovation. I once heard someone say that if Thomas Edison had gone to business school we would all be reading by larger candles."

235.

Only a mediocre executive is always at his best.

In business as in life size up your competition, consider Dave Marr, the famous PGA Golf Champion's quote: "Never bet with anyone you meet on the first tee who has a deep suntan and a one iron in his bag."

Real Leaders Are Remembered For Real Accomplishments

My friend, Wally Amos, who founded "Famous Amos" cookies and "The Uncle Noname Cookie Company", recently gave me an anecdote he lives by and is included in his book "Watermelon Magic: Seeds of Wisdom, Slices of Life". His anecdote really gets you thinking about the meaning of life. Each day all of us work very hard at what we do, but when it's all over, what will people remember about us? Here's Wally's quote:

"Obituaries always list the year you were born and the year you died, separated by a dash, i.e. 1900-1996. When you were born or when you died is not nearly as important as what you did in between— what you put in your dash."

238.

"Broke" can be defined as a temporary situation . . . "Poor" is a state of life.

—Bill Russell

239.

If something is right, it can be done; if it's wrong, it can be done without.

240.

A smart executive will let difficult times make him a better person, not a bitter one.

241.

The conscientious executive arrives early and leaves when it's over!

242.

The true entrepreneur knows that when life gives you scraps, you make a quilt.

243.

Aim at nothing and you can't miss.

244.

A Ferrari doesn't win races . . . the driver does.

245.

Agreement in principle is the politest form of disagreement.

246.

Only make a *great* deal if you have no intention of ever doing business with that person again. Otherwise, make a *good* deal.

247.

Leaders are like shepherds. However, if they take credit for everything, they will only frustrate their flock, who will then seek other shepherds in the organization to lead them to their destination.

248.

Some people dream about fishing and never leave the dock. Others have learned that the more times you cast your net into the water, the better your chances of catching a fish.

249.

No matter how thin you slice it, there are always two sides.

250.

To inherit the future one must be constantly learning. Those who have finished learning will find themselves equipped to live well in the past.

251.

"As long as the mind can envision the fact that you can do something, you can do it."

—Arnold Schwarzenegger

252.

The reason why worry kills more executives than hard work is that more executives worry than work hard.

253.

"Out of intense complexities intense simplicities emerge."

—Albert Einstein

254.

"The truth is always more important than the facts."

—Frank Lloyd Wright

255.

"Now, I'm saying if I've got a goose that can lay a golden egg, then I would study that goose and say 'How can I get it to lay two eggs?'—not, 'Should we have it for Thanksgiving dinner?"

—Ross Perot

256.

Obstacles are things people see when they stop watching their goal

257.

The more sand that escapes from the hourglass of an executive's life, the clearer he should see through it.

258.

Dig where the gold is . . . unless you just need some exercise.

259.

Successful employers seek staff who will do the unusual, who think, and who attract attention by performing more than is expected of them.

—Charles M. Schwab

260.

In corporate life it's interesting to observe that senior executives see everything . . . middle executives suspect everything . . . junior executives know everything.

261.

In business today, too many executives spend money they haven't earned, to buy things they don't need, to impress people they don't even like.

262.

Anyone can climb the ladder of success, but it's the smart executive who makes sure it's leaning against the right building.

263.

If you don't pay attention to your customers, eventually your customers won't pay attention to you.

264.

When checking references, always ask: "Would you hire this person again?" Any answer other than "yes" is a "NO".

265.

Your reputation both precedes and follows you.

266.
A skilled executive can hear what was not being said.

267.
In business, the level of dissension increases geometrically with an increase in the number of issues management must philosophize over.

268.
When nothing seems to help, remember the stone-cutter hammering away at his rock perhaps a hundred times without as much as a crack showing. Yet at the hundred and first blow it will split in two. Know it was not the final blow that did it—- but all that had gone before.

269.
<u>Integrity And Excellence Equal Success</u>

The most exciting time in my entire business career occurred during my years with American Airlines. I had the privilege of working with C. R. Smith, the founder, and in those early days I couldn't wait to get to work. On most days, I worked from 12 to 14 hours a day in an atmosphere charged with energy.

A few years after I started, the company hired a

new CFO named Robert Crandall. Bob certainly fit the company profile . . . he had more energy than anyone I had ever met and did not understand the meaning of "can't do that" . . . it just wasn't in his vocabulary . . . and people quickly learned it should not be in theirs either.

Bob quickly moved into the top marketing spot and ultimately advanced to Chairman of AMR Corporation/ American Airlines. We have been friends for almost 20 years and my respect for him as both and individual and a businessman has never been wavered. He sent me the following inclusion for this book and it is so Bob Crandall, so why he moved forward to become Chairman of American, and so correct for anyone that wants to achieve success that I now share it with you:

"Two of the most important qualities of an outstanding leader are *integrity*—to say what you mean, to deliver what you promise and to stand for what is right—and *excellence*—to be satisfied with no performance short of the best."

270.

If your work ends at five, it's a job. If it goes beyond that time, it's a career.

271.

You Cannot Fly With The Eagles And
Act Like A Canary

Not long ago I was given a copy of Alan Greenberg's book, "Memos From The Chairman." Alan is the Chairman of Bear Stearns Companies and his book is something that everyone in business should read. One day when we were speaking, I asked Alan for a personal anecdote for my book and he faxed me the following:

"Some years ago the bond market dropped considerably. A business reporter from one of the newspapers called me and said they knew Bear Stearns is active in bonds and did we lose any money because of the decline? I told him you cannot fly with the eagles and act like a canary. I believe that."

272.

Most of the time the trip is more exciting than the destination.

273.

The wise executive can make stumbling blocks into stepping stones.

274.

More executives achieve success because they are determined to succeed than because they are destined to succeed.

275.

The greatest thing about the future is that it comes along day by day and allows us the time to influence its outcome.

276.

Efficient planning always costs less than efficient re-acting.

277.

What you are, always speaks louder than what you say.

278.

There are two types of fools: Those who trust everyone and those who trust no one.

279.

Doing the right thing is always more important than doing things right.

280.

Nothing is a greater impediment to being on good terms with others than being ill at ease with yourself.

281.

The more interesting the gossip, the more likely it is to be untrue.

282.

If your company is stupid enough to be run by a committee, be on that committee.

283.

The bitterness of poor quality remains long after the sweetness of meeting the schedule has been forgotten.

284.

Just because you don't get paid more than a baseball player, it doesn't mean you're not as important.

285.

People who will lie for you, will lie to you.

286.

"Well done is always better than well said."

—Benjamin Franklin

287.

You can't control your heritage, but you can control your future.

288.

Some people spend so much time talking about what they have to do, that they don't have enough time to do anything.

289.

"The value of a man should be seen in what he gives and not in what he is able to receive."

—Albert Einstein

290.

"It's not whether you get knocked down. It's whether you get up again."

—Vince Lombardi—Former NFL Coach

291.

Never get drunk with strangers.

292.

In business it's always easier to stay out of trouble than to get out of trouble.

293.

An equal partner should not be someone who brings potential to a venture but someone who stands to lose as much as you when things go wrong.

294.

Don't try to do something cheaply that shouldn't be done at all.

295.

It's not great ideas that succeed, it's great people who make them succeed.

296.

When you can't convince them, confuse them.

297.

Luck is what happens when preparation meets opportunity.

298.

Initiate, Follow Up, Thank And Succeed

A friend of mine, Mort Naiman, is a Director for the Jewish National Fund and recently shared something with me that I also strongly agree with:

"I have found that people who do not wait for

things to happen but initiate them; who stay on top or follow up as a rule; who give proper acknowledgment or thanks; are usually successful in whatever they do."

299.

If you keep doing what you're doing, you'll keep getting what you're getting.

300.

In business, a man should not be judged by what he eats so much as with whom he eats.

301.
Successful People Excel At What They Do

One of the most successful and progressive grocery chains in America is run by one of the best Operating executives in the business . . . I guess that figures doesn't it? Dick Goodspeed, the President and Chief Operating Officer for The Vons Companies, Inc., understands success and sent me a great personal anecdote:

"In these difficult economic times just getting better at what you're doing isn't enough if you really want to succeed. Historically, America has had many competent leaders in all aspects of industry. However, those who succeeded understood that just doing their job wasn't enough. To succeed you must excel at what you do."

302.
It always takes more effort to find out what's right than what's wrong.

303.
Companies that are downsizing should remember that age is important only if you are cheese . . . Integrity, ability and performance are the true measurement of importance.

304.
"I don't know the key to success, but the key to failure is trying to please everybody."

—Bill Cosby

305.
Sometimes when a man with money meets a man with experience, the man with experience ends up with the money and the man with the money ends up with experience.

306.

The concerned investment banker is the one who blows the horn on his Mercedes as he drives through a red light.

307.

To drive your business to success, try to view opportunities through the front windshield and not in the rear view mirror.

308.

Having something to say is always more important than wanting to say something.

309.

The executive who makes no mistakes usually doesn't make anything.

310.

At your child's college graduation you'll never say that you wish you'd spent more time working.

311.

An executive who can't forget is much worse than one who can't remember.

312.

Dumb executives tend to become best friends with other dumb executives.

313.

Even the mighty oak was once a nut.

314.

Try not to work in the same office as someone you once slept with.

315.

Goals without time limits are called wishes . . . Some even call them dreams.

316.

The reason most executives speak about the past is that it is easier to remember where they've been than to figure out where they're going.

317.

Those who have the most demanding bosses are those who are self-employed.

318.

All junior executives should know that if they work hard ten hours a day, every day, they could be promoted to senior executives so that they can work hard for fourteen hours a day.

319.

"You never get ahead of anyone as long as you try to get even with him."

—Lou Holtz

320.

The Ten Commandments Of Street Smarts
By Mark H. McCormack

1. Never underestimate the importance of money . . . It's how business people keep score!

2. Never overestimate the value of money . . . cash is important,but sometimes not as important as respect, thanks, integrity, or the thrill of a job well done.

3. You can never have too many friends in business . . . Given a choice always do business with a friend. It's the best way to leverage your success.

4. Don't be afraid to say, " I don't know" . . . People will respect you much more and will always place more weight on what you do say . . . because they know you're right.

5. Speak less . . . No one ever put their foot in their mouth when they were not speaking. Worse, if you are speaking, you can't be listening and we always learn much more from listening.

6. Keep your promises, the big ones and the little ones . . . both the starting point and the staying point in any business relationship is trust . . . not suspicion. Someone who does what he says he will do will always succeed over a person who doesn't keep his word.

7. Every transaction has a life of its own . . . Some need tender loving care, some need to be hurried away.

8. Commit yourself to quality from day one . . . It's better to do nothing at all than to do something badly.

9. Be nice to people . . . nice gets nice, and all things being equal, courtesy can be very persuasive.

10. Don't hog the credit . . . share it. People will work with you and for you if they are recognized. They will also work against you if they are not.

Editor's Note:

Mark McCormack founded International Management Group (IMG) in 1960, and I have worked with him in a variety of transactions since 1979. He has built IMG into the world's leading organization in the field of athlete representation and sports marketing.

Today, IMG has over 2,000 employees in 71 offices around the world. They represent most of the top superstars in golf, tennis, and many other categories as diverse as classical music.

Additionally, they have become the leading independent producer of television sports programs in the world. Golf Digest has called Mark "the most powerful man in Golf." Tennis Magazine has called him "the most powerful man in Tennis." Sports Illustrated summed it up by describing him simply as "the most powerful man in Sports."

Of equal importance, Mark is the author of many internationally acclaimed best sellers which include: "What They Don't Teach You At Harvard Business School," "The 110% Solution," "Hit The Ground Running," and many others. He is also editor-in-chief of "Success Secrets", one of the best monthly newsletters for anyone who wants to succeed in business.

Mark's astute management and business judgment has probably helped more people achieve success and personal wealth than any other business leader. He is an expert in every phase of the management process including innovative merchandising, licensing, and promotion.

321.
Where you are is important, but not as important as where you are going.

322.

When considering a promotion, remember the difference between an ordinary employee and the extraordinary one is "extra". . . . Most promotions go to the employee who understands that.

323.

A goal is important. If you don't know where you are going, chances are you'll miss it when you get there.

324.

"There are two times in a man's life when he should not speculate—when he cannot afford it, and when he can."

—Mark Twain

325.

"I'm sort of like the old fellow standing by the side of the road. A Cadillac pulled up and the driver asked him if he knew where New Boston was. The old fellow answered, 'No'. The driver asked if he knew where Gladewater was, and the old man said he didn't. The driver then said, 'What in the world do you know?' The old fellow answered, 'I know I'm not lost.' "

—Ross Perot

326.
Always try to do the right thing, unless your conscience tells you otherwise.

327.
The value of a retiring executive should not be measured by his length of service, but by his quality of performance.

328.
Smart executives retire from something to something.

329.
Senior executives can't help getting older, but they certainly don't have to act older.

330.
An army of lions led by a sheep will always be defeated by an army of sheep led by a lion.

331.
If you wish to build a successful company, hire wonderful employees. But remember, employees are like house plants. They require regular care or they will not last.

332.

Most customers vote with their checkbooks whether or not you will stay in business.

333.

When measuring someone's ethics, his behavior is always more telling than his conversation.

334.

Did you ever wonder who ends up with all the paper clips that are used in your office?

335.

The primary benefit of a sharp tongue is that you've always got something handy to cut your own throat.

336.

The world is divided into people who get things done, and people who get the credit.

337.

Plans are nothing–Planning is everything.

—Dwight D. Eisenhower

338.

"Successful executives know that when opportunity doesn't knock, they need to build a door."

—Ted Giannitti, Sr.

339.

To get the right answer, it helps to ask the right question.

340.

In business and in life imaginary difficulties are harder to overcome than real ones.

341.

Always remember that most significant achievements were once considered impossible.

342.

In business, as in life, your chances of being run over are doubled if you stay in the middle of the road.

343.

When your head and your heart are moving in the right direction, chances are your feet are moving in that direction too.

344.

Ever notice how the empty can makes the loudest noise.

345.

There are no shortcuts to any destination worth going to.

346.

Most of the time it is important to get a return *on* your money. Sometimes it's important to just get a return *of* your money.

347.

"When one door closes, another opens; but we often look so long and so regretfully upon the closed door that we do not see the one which has opened for us."

—Alexander Graham Bell

348.

Operating a business with no advertising is like winking at a beautiful woman in the dark . . . You know what you're doing, but nobody else does.

349.

It Takes Great People To Build A Great Business

A person I respect very much is Eileen Ford. She created one of the most successful modeling agencies in the world and launched hundreds of young people into fame and fortune. Eileen was recently telling me how much she liked the snacks that Greenfield Healthy Foods made. (This is the company I founded and later sold to Campbell Soup.) It gave me the opportunity to ask her thoughts about success. She told me:

"I believe success in business is directly related to the quality and character of your staff. I couldn't have built Ford Models, Inc. without the support of my exceptional co-workers, and I would counsel anyone reading John's book to pay particular care in selecting the right people to help you achieve success. In fact, I took so much care that I married my single most important co-worker. I consider myself very blessed to have been able to work with my husband, Jerry, and I know Ford Models wouldn't be the success it is today without him.

350.

"You make more friends by becoming interested in other people than by trying to interest other people in yourself."

—Dale Carnegie

351.

People who are satisfied with their current position will probably stay there. But those who really believe they can do better will always move ahead.

352.

The smart executive knows all the rules so he can break them wisely.

353.

Executives who make a big deal about being right should remember that even a broken clock is right twice a day.

354.

Special interests are called "special" because they have no interest in the general interest.

355.

"Aerodynamically the bumble bee shouldn't be able to fly, but the bumble bee doesn't know it, so it goes on flying anyway."

—Mary Kay Ash

356.

Be an executive who says: "It may be difficult, but it's possible" . . . not one who says: "It may be possible, but it's too difficult."

357.

"If you don't think too good, then don't think too much."

—Ted Williams

358.

"Destiny is not a matter of chance; it is a matter of choice."

—William Jennings Bryan

359.

Quality represents the wisest choice of many alternatives.

360.

Loyalty bought with money can always be overcome with money.

361.

The best way to eliminate any enemy is to make him a friend.

Effort Gets Effort

I receive about ten unsolicited resumes every month from people looking for jobs. They all have the same sort of cover letters . . . Something like "Are you looking for a bright person who increased sales in his last company by 300%?" I always wonder, if this guy's so bright and brought in all that new business, why is he out of a job?

I would like to ask whoever is helping all these people to give them some real world advice:

1. Knock off the hype in the cover letter.

2. Do your homework. Make every letter count. Take a rifle shot not the shotgun approach. Find out everything about the prospect company. What do they do? What do they make? Who runs the company? Where are the offices? What are their problems? Who's their competition?

3. Now write a cover letter that is designed to specifically fit the company and a particular job. Show the reader you think enough of his or her company (and their time) to have done your homework. I will read a letter from someone who took the time to research my business, and if we don't have a position, I will even send the letter to someone I think could use this person's talents. Effort gets effort.

363.

Some executives think the best way to feed the birds is to give more oats to the horses.

364.

Happiness and excellence are directly related. Knowing how to do your job well is directly related to how much you will enjoy doing it.

365.

"Empower the people around you to win . . . and they will make you a winner."

—Michelle Burnett Weir

366.

<u>"When The Pace Of Change Outside An Organization Becomes Greater Than The Pace Of Change Inside The Organization, The End Is Near."</u>

I've been doing business with R.R. Donnelley for quite some time. A number of years ago, John R. Walter was the Chairman and CEO of R.R. Donnelley & Sons, a $6.5 billion dollar publishing company, and was considered one of the America's most successful corporate executives for his ability to recognize and understand those changes that new technology is bringing to our traditional business environments. For example, at Donnelley he anticipated his $2,000 per unit printed encyclopedia business would succumb to a $40 CD-ROM replacement. His assessment was absolutely correct and today Donnelley now produces encyclopedias on CD-ROM. Recently, John accepted the position of President at AT&T. He sent me the above maxim and his other thoughts pertaining to the business changes that we will see in the 21st Century. Changes that all business executives must recognize and react to or suffer huge consequences. Technology is moving so fast within some industries and the penalties for wrong decisions are becoming very unforgiving. John correctly said "Only leaders will carry on—the followers will cease to exist." Businesses that are being impacted by great technological changes must now operate with a heightened sense of urgency. Such companies can no longer enjoy the luxury of time intensive research studies and learning curves. As John Walter believes, "We need to build a culture in which we expect to make some mistakes, learn from them and quickly apply everything we learn." John also believes that the pace of change is moving so fast that not only are segments of industry being flattened but entire industries are being impacted. The old adage: "Ready, Aim, Fire" is being replaced by: "Fire, Aim, Fire, Aim, Fire" as industry realizes that speed to market can only be accomplished by a short burst into the market, evaluate what happens, make corrections and go back in with a bigger approach. My stock tip for readers of this book: With John Walter moving to the top of AT&T, buy their stock.

367.
Question Enough And You Will Find The Answer

I was playing squash the other night with Ted Giannitti and he told me the amazing story of Stanislavsky Lech who saved his own life by constantly questioning until he found the answer.

Stanislavsky and his family were arrested by the Nazis during World War II and sent to a death camp in Krakow. His entire family was shot in front of him and he was forced into hard labor.

Starving to death he somehow continued, but he knew if he didn't escape he would surely die. He questioned how to succeed every minute of every day. His friends told him it was useless. He should simply pray, but he refused to accept this and continued to question . . . continued to search for a solution.

Finally, the solution presented itself. The Germans would pile bodies next to the gas chambers and each day load them into trucks to be dumped into mass graves.

As his work day ended, Lech slipped out of line, ducked behind a truck loaded with bodies, removed his clothing and, while no one was looking, jumped into the back of the truck with the dead. More bodies were dumped on top of him and he lay quiet, pretending to be dead.

Finally the truck moved outside the camp grave site and dumped its awful cargo. Lech stayed silent for hours until dark and then ran naked over 25 miles to freedom.

Why did Lech survive? Because he refused to give up. More important, he continuously questioned to find a solution.

In business, if something isn't right, we have two choices: accept it or question it to find a solution. Sometimes you have got to ask many questions to find the right answer. The key is to never stop questioning until you are satisfied with the answer.

368.
Most senior executives spend the second half of their lives recovering from the first half.

369.
The future belongs to the learned, not to the historian.

370.

Sometimes A Simple " Thank You" Is The Best Course Of Action

I recently had the opportunity to communicate with Roger and Paul Sonnabend who run Sonesta International Hotels. Paul gave me a personal story which I have included in my book as it represents something that's happened to most of us who travel.

"Last month I took the sleeper train from New York to Chicago. I explained to the porter when I arrived in Chicago that I had not been on a sleeper train for many years. I wanted to tip him but did not know what was an appropriate amount, so I asked him what his average tip was. He told me $10.00—I gave him the money and commented that he must do quite well. He replied, I don't hit my average very often!"

371.

If you lie down in the face of conflict, someone will surely walk over you.

372.

If you don't keep doing it better, a competitor will.

373.

"Life is something that happens to you while you are making other plans."

—Barbara Biderman, Marriott Hotels

374.

Anyone who accepts "good enough" as their work standard should know that such a standard isn't good enough at all.

375.

Successful executives have learned to pay more attention to what employees actually do rather than to what they say they'll do.

376.

<u>Don't Ever Underestimate Your Customer</u>

Consumers are really very smart. When you reduce the quality of your product to save a buck they really do notice . . . and usually they also save a buck . . . they stop buying your product.

377.

Extremely successful executives should know that those moments which are absolutely free from worry are called panic.

"Never Underestimate The Value Of Change"

Certain industries are more sensitive to change than others. The history books are full of companies that were blind sided by change and went out of business. One classic example is the Best Buggy Whip Company that woke up one morning out of business because Henry Ford invented a thing called the car and people stopped buying buggies. I guess it was good for the horses but I wouldn't want to be an investor in a buggy whip company. If I were in the retail photo film development business, I would also be looking over my shoulder . . . here comes digital cameras that don't use film! William A. Franke, the Chairman, President and Chief Executive Officer at America West Airlines, obviously, knows about the challenges of change in his industry. He gave me his advice which covers the subject perfectly:

"Never underestimate the value of change. The sphere of business is in constant motion, and those who aren't able to anticipate and adapt quickly find themselves left behind. You can never become satisfied with complacency or comfortable with the status quo. You have to anticipate change and learn to manage it. Not just react to it, but actively cultivate it. Expect change, be challenged by it, and you'll rarely be surprised by it."

I would recommend that every CEO in America share Bill Franke's quote with their staff . . . every day!

379.

"You know . . . we talk a lot about *numbers*. But our business is about *people*. And taking care of them. Our own . . . and our customers. If we take good care of our people . . . they'll take good care of our customers. And the rest will come."

—Larry Stone

Executive Vice President

Lowe's

380.

In contract law a completion date should be defined as the point at which liquidated damages begin.

381.

Been There . . . Done That

I have known Gerry Roche, the Chairman of Heidrick & Struggles for more than a decade. Gerry heads up one of the best executive search firms in the world and once gave me a maxim that makes great sense:

"You can no more tell somebody to do something that you ain't done, than you can come back from someplace where you ain't been."

382.

When traveling abroad, it is best to remember that money, not English, is the international language.

383.

Don't piss off a crocodile until after you've crossed the river.

384.

In business, as in life, the worst itches are always in spots where you don't want the public to see you scratching.

385.

Modesty Is Far More Impressive

At a luncheon with photographer Yousuf Karsh and his wife, Neil Armstrong, the astronaut who became the first human to set foot on the moon, politely asked the couple about the many places they had visited. Mr. Karsh responded: "Mr. Armstrong, you've walked on the moon. We would much rather hear about your travels." "But that's the only place I've ever been," remarked Armstrong, apologetically.

386.

The most important thing that keeps most people from becoming successful is hard work.

387.

"In most construction proposals a bid is a wild guess carried out to two decimal places."

—Ted Giannitti, Sr.

388.

It is never too late to become what you might have become.

389.

<u>More People Get Into Trouble For Things They Say Rather Than For What They Do</u>

General Westmoreland called down to the base motor pool one day and asked what vehicles were on the base and available. The Private who answered the call said: "Two jeeps, one truck and one sedan for the stupid General." Not believing what he just heard, the General asked the Private: "Do you know who you're talking to?" The Private said: "No". "Well, this is General Westmoreland." The Private thought for a moment—highly aware of his incredible blunder—and asked: "Well, do you know who you're talking to?" The General responded "No, I don't", to which the Private said: "Well, so long, stupid" and hung up the phone.

390.

Ninety percent of the time things will turn out worse than you expect. The other ten percent of the time you had no right to expect so much.

391.

To Survive In Business You Must Be Able To Think And Act Quickly

A story circulated around Wall Street a while ago about a tough chairman of a major company who stopped into the famous restaurant, "21", for a quick bite. Not being too hungry, he asked the waiter for half of a sirloin steak. Normally the waiter would simply have told him they didn't serve half steaks, but given the importance of this customer, the waiter agreed and left for the kitchen. Unbeknownst to the waiter, the chairman followed him to the kitchen to tell him he wanted the steak rare. As the waiter announced to the chef, "I need half a steak for a real jerk," he noticed the chairman standing behind him and, without missing a stroke, continued to comment to the chef, "and the other half goes to this gentleman."

The Race To Success Has No Finish Line

You can usually pick those companies with exceptional leadership simply by observing the quality of their products or service.

Victor H. Doolan, the President of BMW, participated in my first book several years ago and he recently gave me one of his personal success maxims that I wanted to share in this book: "For us there is no finish line."

As a very long time BMW customer I can honestly tell you that this company has no finish line . . . every year their product gets better and better.

Victor Doolan represents the poster child for any leader that strives for excellence. His attitude keeps BMW at the leading edge and his philosophy of "no finish line" is one of the best maxims any CEO can share with his or her fellow employees.

393.

The critical path method is a management technique for losing your shirt under perfect control.

Necessity Is The Mother Of Invention

In 1981, we moved to a home located in a large wooded area in Connecticut. One morning I spotted a man walking around the side of our house. Thinking he was a prowler, I approached the man slowly with my .38 cal handgun. As it turned out, I almost shot the electric company meter reader. So I decided to buy a device that I could put at the beginning of my driveway that would alert me if someone was coming. I found that the only sensors available required a wire to be run underground from the end of the driveway to the house. Since my driveway was well over 1,000 feet long, the cost to install a system was $2,500. I saw an opportunity and hired an electrical engineer to make me a prototype of a radio operated driveway detector. Once we had perfected the prototype, I formed a company to market driveway detectors and struck a contract with a major alarm manufacturer to produce our products. After the first year, we had sales in the hundreds of thousands of dollars and I was approached by another company to sell my business. I sold out for $300,000 and still collect royalties to this day.

395.

A dog that can count to ten is a remarkable dog . . . not a great mathematician.

396.

Usually the last ten percent of the performance sought generates one-third of the cost and two-thirds of the problems.

397.

There Are Always Two Sides To Every Story

When asked his opinion on a play that did not receive great reviews, Oscar Wilde, the famous British Writer, once commented: "The play was wonderful . . . the audience was a disaster."

398.

"Don't build me a watch, just tell me the time."

—Charlie McCarthy
Chief Operating Officer
Tetley USA

399.
You Rarely Get Into Trouble When You Keep Your Mouth Shut

More people in business get into trouble for saying the wrong thing to the wrong people at the wrong time. There's a great Mark Twain tale that makes this point. Mark once spent three weeks in Maine fishing during the closed season. On his return to New York in the lounge car of the train, with his illegal catch on ice in the baggage car, he struck up a conversation with a stranger to relate the story of his successful fishing exploit. The stranger's expression grew more grim with each of Twain's boasts. Finally, Twain asked: "By the way, who are you?" "I'm the State Game Warden" was the unwelcome reply. "And who are you?" Twain, nearly white with fright, answered: "Well, to be totally truthful, Warden, I'm the biggest damned liar in the whole United States."

400.
If a sufficient number of management layers are stacked on top of each other, it can be assured that disaster is not left to chance.

401.
The meek might inherit the earth, but the strong will always retain the mineral rights.

402.
Negotiation At Its Best

J.P. Morgan was interested in buying a pearl pin. The jeweler he approached found the perfect pin and sent it in a box to Morgan with a bill for $5,000. The following day the box was returned with a note from Morgan: "I like the pin, but I don't like the price. If you will accept the enclosed check for $4,000, please send back the box which is sealed with the seal unbroken." The enraged jeweler returned the check to the messenger and dismissed him in anger. He opened the box to remove the pin only to find that it had already been replaced with a check from Morgan for $5,000.

403.

"Farming looks mighty easy when your plow is a pencil and you're a thousand miles from a cornfield."

—Dwight D. Eisenhower

404.
Leaders Must Be Good Communicators

Most of the world's finest and most successful companies are run by leaders who understand the value of good communication. Leaders who never leave their office . . . who never communicate with their organizations will never see their companies achieve their maximum potential.

Ron Allen, the Chairman, President and Chief Executive Officer of Delta Air Lines recently gave me one of his observations on the value of good communications and it is so correct that I would like to share it with you:

"Leaders must be good communicators. It is always easier to lead when your organization is already going the same way you are."

405.

Decisions reduce anxiety.

406.

The wise executive never shoots a messenger bringing bad news because, after a while, all he'll receive is the good news.

407.

If you think you can, you can. And if you think you can't, you're right.

408.

"If you're right you just hang in there, stand your ground and don't give an inch. If you have the will to do that, at some point the tide will turn."

—Ross Perot

409.
<u>The Truth Be Known!</u>

At a political dinner the famous newspaper columnist, Ann Landers, was introduced to a rather pompous Senator. "So, you're Ann Landers," he drawled. "Say something funny." Without hesitation Ann replied: "Well, you're a politician . . . . tell me a lie."

410.
Nothing is more rewarding than to watch someone who says it can't be done get interrupted by someone actually doing it.

411.
"If your time is too precious to give to your friends or family . . . change your lifestyle."

—Peter Capozzi

412.
The exceptional manager will always expect that the expected can be prevented, and that the unexpected should have been expected.

The Three Most Important Actions To Building A Successful Business Are: Focus, Focus, And Focus

In real estate it's location, location and location, but when building a business, the key is focus. Focus allows you to constantly be on top of both opportunities and problems. Opportunities come and go quickly. If you are not focused, the opportunity will go right by and you will never know it. Given sufficient time, small problems tend to become big problems and strong business focus allows you time to explore the "little things." C.R. Smith, the Founder of American Airlines, once told me: "Worry about the small things . . . the big things will take care of themselves." If you are not focused, you never have time to get into the "small things."

I recently had dinner with one of my closest friends, Jon Dawson, who founded Dawson-Samberg. Jon chastised me for not being totally focused. His firm is one of the best money management companies in America. With capital over $2 billion and annual returns on many of his funds over 30%, you would think Jon would take life easier. Not so. He is constantly on the road visiting new companies and looking for great investments. This guy is totally focused and the returns he provides his investors show it. I know he considers me something of an anomaly because I always have new business opportunities under development and it would appear that I am not totally focused on any one of them. I thought about his dinner comments and realized that finding new opportunities is what I do. That's my business. That's my focus. I chose early in my career that I would hire the best people I could find to run my companies, and my challenge is to be sure *they* stay focused on the day to day problems and opportunities.

414.
The Power Of Positive Thinking

Nothing upsets me more than an employee who immediately starts telling me why something won't work. If we spend two hours in a meeting discussing why something won't work, that's two hours we could have spent trying to identify how to make something work. The good manager will be alert to negative thinkers and will build positive responses to move negative employees back on track. For example, when someone says: "We've never done that before", you answer: "We have a great opportunity to be first." "We already tried that", can be answered with: "What did we learn from our previous experience that will allow us to try again?" "We'll cannibalize our existing sales", should be answered with: "Let's increase our business and develop programs to protect against cannibalization". "We don't have the expertise" should be answered with: "Let's find the expertise to make this work". "Our customers won't go for it" should be answered with: "Let's show our customers some new opportunities". "Our product is good enough" should be countered with: "Let's try to improve our product before our competition does." In my experience negative thinkers drive negative bottom lines. Businesses are built with positive thinkers.

415.
"If it looks like a duck, walks like a duck, and quacks like a duck, chances are it's a duck."

—Sen. Edward Kennedy

416.
If someone says something unkind about you, live your life so that no one will believe it.

417.
Take Risks

Not long ago, I had dinner with Jim Burke. We were supporting a "One to One" function for our mutual friend, Ray Chambers, and we got into a discussion about taking risks in business. Jim told me a wonderful story that I would like to share with you:

Jim Burke became the head of a new products group at Johnson & Johnson. One of his first products was a children's chest rub. It failed miserably and Jim believed he would be fired when he was called into the Chairman's office. However, to his surprise Mr. Johnson asked if he was the one who just cost the company a lot of money and then added. "Well, I want to congratulate you. If you made a mistake it means you took a risk, and if we don't take risks we will never grow. That is what business is all about." Years later Jim Burke became the Chairman of Johnson & Johnson.

418.
A union strike is like trying to increase the egg production by strangling the chicken.

419.
If you know how, you'll always have a job. If you know why, you'll be the boss.

420.
Any problem you can solve with a check isn't a problem, it's an expense.

421.

Never let what you can't do interfere with what you can do.

422.

Remember, in business committees may keep minutes . . . but they usually cost the company hours.

423.

"Nobody goes there anymore because it's too crowded."

—Yogi Berra

424.

"All good things come to him who waits . . . . as long as he works like hell while he waits."

—Philine van Lidth de Jeude

If It Works . . . No Problem

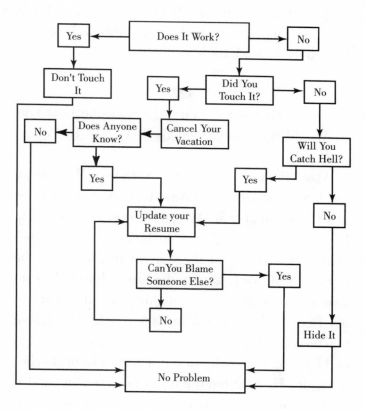

Everyone is surrounded by opportunities, but they only exist once they have been seen. They will only be seen if they are looked for, and they will only be looked for if you have a goal to achieve.

Never Do Or Say Something To Someone That You Would Not Want Them To Do Or Say To You

About ten years ago, I sat next to Dom Rossi in an airplane from Detroit to New York. At that time, he was President of N.W. Ayer, the oldest and one of the largest advertising agencies in the world. We have become "brothers" over the years. Our kids go to the same school, we belong to the same church, he's an owner in several of my companies and sits on one of my Boards. I respect him very much. The above maxim is one I have taught my children all their lives and I am honored to know it is a maxim Dom also believes in. He sent me the following anecdote and if everyone in business lived by it, the world would be a much better place:

"A long time ago, I was sitting at a recreation league basketball game with a group of teenage friends. There was an elderly janitor sweeping the area adjacent to the court, and several of the kids started to call him names and have fun at his expense.

I asked one of the kids if he would be doing this if the man who was the target of their insensitive behavior was his grandfather. He responded quickly, "Of course not!", stopped, thought for a moment about what he just said, and told his friends to stop. They did.

My Mom taught me the above maxim when I was a young boy and I have followed it carefully throughout my entire business career. I know it has served me well, and I hope everyone who reads this book stops for a moment, like my teenage friend did at our basketball game, to reflect on their interpersonal skills which are so important if one wishes to succeed in business today."

428.

People who strike out at someone when they get angry should be careful not to strike themselves.

429.

All who snore are not always sleeping

430.

In any new business overvalue the negative projections by two. Undervalue the positive projections by half.

Solve The Objection To Make A Sale

A few years ago, a good friend asked me to help his son who owned a pet store that wasn't doing very well. The boy sold the usual dogs, cats, fish, turtles, pet food and miscellaneous related supplies. At first I resisted getting involved since I didn't have a background in pet retailing and I also felt that if the boy went out of business after I gave him my advice, I would probably lose my friendship with his father.

Since this was a good friend, my desire to help won out over my better judgment. I went down to the store and met with the boy. The location was okay . . . It could have been better, but to upgrade is a function of available expense dollars which he didn't have. He was just about breaking even.

I reviewed each of his revenue categories and stopped at fish. He had a lot of inventory dollars tied up in fish, tanks, filters, food and the like. He told me he was going to discontinue selling fish because it wasn't making money and the upkeep (cleaning the tanks) was too time consuming. I thought about it for a minute and asked him what he thought the biggest customer objection was to buying pet fish. "Cleaning the tank" was the instant reply.

In sales you must always solve the prospects' objections before making a sale. Based on this premise, I developed a plan.

My suggestion was to produce an inexpensive direct mail brochure which highlighted all the obvious and not so obvious benefits of having pet fish. It was not directed to the general public, but to professional and business prospects like doctors, lawyers, clothing stores, restaurants, and other locations that had either a waiting room or lots of public traffic. The key to the new program was to rent the fish and the tanks by the month and, most important, come in each week to clean the tank for a fee. If a fish died, we would replace it at no cost.

Over the next three months alone we signed 42 rental contracts, and established enough cleaning revenue ($20 per week) to cover almost the entire annual rent of the pet store.

Most important, hundreds of people saw the store name on fish tanks all around the area and the publicity generated tremendous exposure and new sales for the store.

432.

Any man who wants to hang himself can always find a noose.

433.

In business, as in fishing, trouble starts when you open your mouth.

434.

Eagles don't hunt flies.

435.

If you're skating on thin ice, skate real fast.

436.

Old wolves may lose their teeth but never their nature.

437.

To finish sooner, take your time.

438.

Working hard to succeed is always better than working a little to fail.

439.

If you are constantly looking back, chances are pretty good you'll fall into a hole ahead.

440.

The Less Baggage The Easier The Ride

Wally Amos once said: "My experiences have shown me that life truly is a journey, and the less baggage we carry the easier the ride." I also define baggage as doing business with people you don't like, don't trust, or just find annoying. Clearly, that isn't always possible, but consider how great it would be to go through a day only speaking to people you truly enjoy.

A goal should be to try to cut back on anything negative so all you have left are the positives.

441.

"If you have tried to do something but couldn't, you are far better off than if you had tried to do nothing and succeeded."

—John T. Ragland, Jr.

442.

"Learn to profit from your mistakes . . . If you can't, your competition will."

—Eric Klar

443.

Making a living should never be confused with making a life.

444.

Man is not the creature of circumstances. Circumstances are the creatures of man.

445.

"Experience is not what happens to a man; it is what man does with what happens to him."

—Aldous Huxley

446.

"We first make our habits, and then our habits make us."

—John Dryden

447.

"Be more concerned with your character than your reputation, because your character is what you really are, while your reputation is merely what others think you are."

—John Wooden

448.

To be very successful, hold yourself to a higher standard than your boss expects of you.

449.

"If we did all the things we are capable of doing, we would literally astound ourselves."

—Thomas Edison

450.

Wealth is a by-product of a man's ability to think.

451.

The tiny point of a quick pen is the sharpest weapon known to man.

—Eveline van Lidth de Jeude

452.

"Measure twice . . . cut once"

—Ross Perot

453.

"We act as though comfort and luxury were the chief requirements of life, when all that we need to be really happy is something to be enthusiastic about."

—Charles Kingsley

454.

"A leader is best when people barely know that he leads. Not so good when people obey and acclaim him. Worst when they despise him . . . but a good leader, when his work is done, his aim fulfilled, they will all say, "We did this ourselves."

—Lao Tzu

455.

The race is not always won by the fastest runner but sometimes by those who just keep running.

456.

A turn in the road is not the end of the road unless you fail to make the turn.

457.

Take care of your customers or your competition will.

458.

"When given a choice . . . take both."

—Peter Rogers
Former Chairman Nabisco Foods

459.

Experience is a good teacher but she sends terrific bills.

460.

Aim for the top . . . There's more room there.

461.

If your business isn't moving fast enough consider the turtle . . . It can't move at all if it doesn't stick its neck out.

462.

Given a choice between building your business on large debt or facing a firing squad . . . choose the firing squad. There's a chance the firing squad might miss.

463.

It is always better to make payroll than to collect a paycheck.

464.

Act successful if you want to be successful.

465.

You can't shake hands with a clenched fist.

466.

If you must do it by the book, be the author.

Every new cadet at West Point is required to commit
Major General Schofield's Definition of Discipline to
memory.

As relevant to corporate management as to the mili-
tary, it is interesting that given the increasing
equalitarian level of modern day society, it is even
more relevant today than it was in 1879.

Schofield's Definition of Discipline

The discipline which make the
soldiers of a free country reliable in
battle is not to be gained by harsh or
tyrannical treatment. On the contrary,
such treatment is far more likely to
destroy than to make an army. It is
possible to impart instruction and
to give commands in such a manner
and such a tone of voice to inspire
in the soldier no feeling but an intense
desire to obey, while the opposite
manner and tone of voice cannot fail
to excite strong resentment and a desire
to disobey. The one mode or the other
of dealing with subordinates springs
from a corresponding spirit in the breast
of the commander. He who feels the respect
which is due to others cannot fail to inspire

in them regard for himself, while he who feels, and hence manifests, disrespect toward others, especially his inferiors, cannot fail to inspire hatred against himself.

—Major General John M. Schofield
in an address to the Corps of Cadets
August 11, 1879

468.
Strong Roots Make Strong Trees

One of the kindest people I have ever met is Craig Rydin, the President of Godiva Chocolate. He is one of the those few people everyone describes as "what a nice guy." He doesn't even get mad at me when I beat him at tennis! He recently sent me the following anecdote, and it is so typically Craig Rydin that I wanted to share it with you:

"In 1964 I took a job at a small department store in the rural mill town of Berlin, New Hampshire.

The store was run by two generations of owners. My career started as a floor washer and trash remover. I was promoted to stock boy a short time later. I then moved up to sales and ran the annual sidewalk sale. Ultimately, I earned the right to manage much of the business. The owners personified the results of hard work, impeccable values, and the ability to interrelate with people irrespective of their backgrounds or where they came from. My early work experience provided me with a foundation and values that have allowed me to achieve excellence in my business career.

Today, I no longer work in the small rural mill-town of Berlin, New Hampshire. I am privileged to lead one of the world's greatest brands, Godiva. I am also privileged to share with my employees the same lessons and values I learned from the owners of Rydin's Department Store, and I can't thank these owners enough for the strong roots they have given me . . . Thank you Mom and Dad very much!"

469.

Make sure that the cost of the insurance doesn't exceed the cost of the accident.

470.
If You Don't Ask . . . You Don't Get

It seems there was a pretzel stand out front of an office building in New York. One day a man came out of the building, plunked down a quarter, and then went on his way without taking a pretzel. This happened every day for three weeks. Finally, the old lady running the stand spoke up: "Sir, excuse me. May I have a word with you?" The fellow said: "I know what you're going to say. You're going to ask me why I give you a quarter every day and don't take a pretzel." And the woman said: "Not at all. I just want to tell you the price is now 35 cents."

—William Schreyer
Former Chairman
Merrill Lynch

471.
In any battle, the best armor is to keep out of range.

472.
Trust Your Instincts

Not long ago at a One To One Dinner, Bill Russell, who I think is the greatest basketball player to every play the game and an amazing person, told me the following story and his morale is one that I live by every day:

"When I was in the 11th grade, I was cut from the junior varsity basketball team (really smart coach!). Our varsity coach then approached me and asked me to play on the varsity team. "I just got cut from the JV Team", I said. His answer: "I'm not coaching the JV." The moral of this story is to go with your instincts and you may just be right.

473.

The truly happy person is the one who can enjoy the scenery even when he must take a detour.

474.

Executives who take cold showers in the morning start the day much more alert. They are also incredible jerks.

475.

"Some men see things and say why? I dream of things that never were and ask, Why not?"

—John F. Kennedy

476.

"Business is like dogsledding. if you are *not* the lead dog, your view will always be the same."

—Bernal Quiros

477.

<u>Respect Your Employees And They Will Respect Your Business</u>

Some people get it right most of the time and others don't even have a clue. Dick Fogarty, Former Chairman and CEO of Labatt USA, is one who really understands building a business. He was up to see me recently and told me the following:

"When I was younger and new to the business world, I was totally impatient with idle chatter and anything that got in the way of moving the business forward. At that time, I was somewhat taken back by my division head occasionally *walking the floor* to chat with everyone from the mail room clerk to the senior managers, and it usually wasn't about business! It was a friendly hello, a pat on the back, a word of encouragement, or perhaps something about the family. It seemed like wasted time to me, but eventually I figured it out. It was all about care, recognition and respect; it was all about running a business well. Executives who don't understand that their employees are their greatest asset will never achieve their maximum success."

As an aside to this story, the principal of Columbus-Magnet School in Norwalk, sits and has lunch every day with an individual student, doing just what Dick Fogarty does. Columbus was recently voted the best grade school in Connecticut.

478.

Remember to dig deep when interviewing someone for a key position. Just as a wise man can say a foolish thing, a fool can say something wise once in awhile.

479.
<u>Try To Earn What The Job Is Worth</u>

Recently I had lunch with a close friend who was leaving a senior position at a major Fortune 500 Company. He had been with this company for 17 years and had never gone through "the job search" process. Over the course of two hours we talked about every aspect of finding a new job. At one point I told him my philosophy about compensation is to be paid what the job is worth. I strongly believe companies could reduce significant employee turnover if they simply paid their people a fair and correct compensation. I also believe if someone is rude enough to ask you your current salary, you have the right to be rude enough to tell him the number you "think" the job is really worth. What you are earning at your current position is totally your business and the management at a new prospective company really has no right to even ask about your current financial affairs. The interviewer should know what "his or her" job is worth and should tell you the amount they are willing to pay you based upon the scope and responsibilities of their job and your resume experience. I counseled my friend to mention a salary that he thought the new position was worth if the situation arose, knowing his current company would never give out confidential compensation information to any outsiders for verification.

About two weeks later, I received a huge basket of fruit from my friend. I called him thinking it was a thanks for taking two hours of my time, but he told me it was for my specific advice. As it turned out he did well on a job interview with the President of a new company and was offered a position. The President then asked him what his "current" salary was. Remembering our lunch conversation, my friend gave him a number he believed his new job was really worth, which was about $100,000 more than he was currently making. The President thought for a moment and said: "Okay, the position is well within that range, and I can also give you an additional 30% as an incentive to join us."

480.
"Worry About The Small Things . . . The Big Things Will Take Care Of Themselves."

In the 1960's, Mr. C.R. Smith, the founder of American Airlines, gave me the above maxim. I was working at LaGuardia Airport on Christmas morning and Mr. Smith came out to thank everyone for working on the holiday. I wonder how many senior executives would do that today?

I have tried to live my business career following Mr. Smith's maxim, and it seems my biggest problems always occur when I don't adhere to it.

My wife and I recently held a party at our home to honor our friend, Michael Bolton, for the work he's doing helping high risk inner city children. The Governor issued a special proclamation to recognize Michael and our Mayor presented him with a "Key to the City." We had almost 60 corporate Presidents and their spouses attending. I took care of all the "big" things: great catering, a valet service to park cars and, given the level of importance of all our guests, security guards both in and out of uniform. One uniformed police officer was stationed at the front gate with a guest list to check guests in as they arrived . . . and then a "small thing" happened. Since the party was honoring Michael Bolton, I didn't list him on the guard's guest list. When Michael arrived, the guard would not let him in. The house is almost a 1/4 mile from the end of the driveway so there was no way I could know what was going on. Fortunately, Michael is one of the more resourceful people I know and he convinced the guard he really was invited and to let him in.

In Business, As In Life, The Will To Succeed Can Overcome Anything

In 1982, a 16 year old Canadian, Silken Laumann, took up rowing for the first time. Two years later she earned a bronze medal for Canada in the Los Angeles Olympics. By the end of 1991, she was the World Champion and World Record Holder in the Single Scull.

Just ten weeks prior to the 1992 Olympics, two German Scullers accidentally rammed their bow into Silken's right leg severing five muscle groups and shattering her tibia as well as her dream to win the Women's Single Scull.

Secretly, Silken began weight lifting in her hospital bed. After five operations she began to row again. Unbelievably, in just two months after her accident, she competed in Barcelona. Halfway through the race she was in fourth place and in tremendous agony. She reached inside and, telling herself she could overcome the pain, she inched forward, refusing to let up. She took third place, winning a Bronze Medal which, under the circumstances, was nothing short of miraculous.

In 1995, she won the Single's event at the Pan American Games and took a Silver Medal in the 1996 Olympics in Atlanta.

All of us in business should look at this young lady's accomplishment as our motivation to succeed no matter how difficult the situation might seem to be. She is living proof that the human spirit can overcome anything if the will is strong enough.

482.

When considering a new job, review what you've got to do for eight hours and ask yourself how you'd feel if you had to do it for a lifetime.

483.

Even if your entire Board of Directors votes for a stupid idea, it's still a stupid idea.

484.

Having it all doesn't necessarily mean having it all at once.

485.

Temper gets you in trouble. Pride keeps you there.

486.

Many people don't look dumb until they start talking.

487.

Before borrowing money from a friend, decide which you need most.

488.

If the water is real murky, only a fool would dive right in.

489.

Mediocre people tend to hire mediocre people.

490.

There's never a right way to do a wrong thing.

491.

"The best executive is the one who has sense enough to pick good men to do what he wants done, and self-restraint enough to keep from meddling with them while they do it."

—Theodore Roosevelt

492.

Striving for excellence is motivating; striving for perfection is demoralizing.

493.

Retirement is that period in life when "time is no longer money."

494.

If you spend too much time at work and put your marriage on the back burner, it is only a matter of time before your marriage will boil over.

495.

Executives who resist change because they think they're on the right track should remember they can get run over if they just stand there.

496.

Solve The Need To Be Successful

In the late 1990's statistics showed that the free standing insert (FSI) also known as Sunday Newspaper Coupons to the average consumer, was one of the most inefficient marketing tools available to the consumer package goods industry. It only represented a 2% redemption. This means that 98% of the marketers money was wasted. But what else was available for a brand manager to drive consumer trial?

A man named Jon Robertson came to see me with an idea: To capture supermarket consumer transaction data directly at the register and know who bought what and when. Then use that data to target coupon offerings to exactly the right consumer at exactly the right time. For example, if someone who last month purchased Pampers just received a coupon to purchase Johnson's Baby Powder, the odds are far better than 2% that Johnson's would make a sale.

Kitty Litter would get a much better response if they only sent their coupons to folks who bought cat food within the past 30 days.

Robertson had identified both the problem and the solution, but execution was a completely different matter.

I funded the primary capital to develop the initial business proposition and plan. We then raised a due diligence fund from senior executives in the fields of retail grocery, consumer package goods manufacturing, computer technology, and information research. This "value added" group of senior executives became our core leadership group and allowed us to leap forward with amazing speed.

Rather than fund the hardware and software required (which is always changing) we entered into relationships with IBM, NCR and others who would benefit from our business and allow us to operate as a "virtual corporation." The capital or technology risks associated with a business in constant tech transition would be born by others.

The business provided a win, win, win, win combination. The consumer gets great discounts; the retailer (supermarket) gets incremental revenue, state of the art technology and a better lock on his customers; the manufacturer gets a much more efficient promotional tool and, lastly, we have an amazingly profitable business.

497.

"Life is funny; if you refuse to accept nothing but the best, you very often get it."

—Somerset Maugham

498.

Spend the extra dollars to maintain your equipment. Remember, you don't have to brush all your teeth either . . . only the ones you want to keep.

499.

If you're in charge and you stop rowing, don't be surprised if the rest of your crew stops too.

500.

Decisions should not be made because they are easy, cheap, or because everyone agrees. They should only be made because they are right